# ChurchMarketing 101

Preparing Your Church for Greater Growth

# Richard L. Reising

BakerBooks

Grand Rapids, Michigan

Published by Baker Books
a division of Baker Publishing Group
P.O. Box 6287, Grand Rapids, MI 49516-6287
www.bakerbooks.com

Second printing, May 2006

Printed in the United States of America

Library of Congress Cataloging-in-Publication Data
Reising, Richard, 1972–
    ChurchMarketing 101 : preparing your church for greater growth / Richard Reising.
        p.    cm.
    Includes bibliographical references.
    ISBN 10: 0-8010-6592-5 (pbk.)
    ISBN 978-0-8010-6592-7 (pbk.)
    1. Church marketing. I. Title: ChurchMarketing one hundred one. II. Title: ChurchMarketing one hundred and one. III. Title: Church marketing 101. IV. Title.
    BV652.23.R45  2006
    254—dc22                                                                    2005023437

Published in association with the literary agency of Alive Communications, Inc., 7680 Goddard Street, Suite 200, Colorado Springs, CO 80920.

"Richard Reising gets the power of a brand! His perspectives on today's cultural perceptions of the church are extremely insightful. Church leaders need to read this book."

Darren Whitehead, director of Next Gen Ministries,
Willow Creek Community Church

"Richard Reising approaches the subject of church marketing with the brilliance of a businessman and the passion of a pastor. Required reading for every pastor in America."

Brad Abare, founder of Personality™ and the
Center for Church Communication

"Jesus challenged his followers not to marginalize their influence but rather to leverage their light for maximum reach. This is the essence of church and ministry marketing. Richard Reising has done a great service to all who are interested in increasing the influence of the gospel by writing *ChurchMarketing 101*. He is repelled by marketing based on hype or half-truths. Richard Reising calls us to market the ministry in our stewardship truthfully, biblically, and undergirded by a clear mission. You will finish this book with a clearer head and a hotter heart!"

Dr. David Shibley, president, Global Advance

"As a pastor of a 13,000 member church, I can testify that 'church marketing' is *not* an oxymoron. Every church has a reputation in its community. Richard Reising has given us a tremendous advantage by writing how every church can enhance its effectiveness in sharing the claims of Jesus Christ. This book is a must-read for anyone who is committed to reaching their community with the gospel."

Dr. David Dykes, author, pastor, Green Acres Baptist Church, Tyler, Texas

"Reising converts lofty corporate marketing strategies into simple, Christ-centered and people-focused principles. I can see its role in increasing the effectiveness and connectedness of both church and ministry. Any organization will take away a clearer sense of vision and a greater understanding of how to get there."

Dave Dravecky, bestselling author and founder of Outreach of Hope

"The church is the hope of the world. *ChurchMarketing 101* reveals the principles necessary to focus the message of Christ like a laser at targeted groups. Richard Reising has an important message for the church to hear and apply."

Robert Morris, senior pastor, Gateway Church, Southlake, Texas

"In his work *ChurchMarketing 101* we meet a man passionate about his vision, not a vision for marketing but a vision for so much more. Richard Reising has a heart for the church because he has a heart for the church's task of reaching others with the gospel of Jesus Christ. Richard does not take a cookie-cutter approach to marketing, but makes every effort to establish a biblical approach as to how to grow a healthy church on its own terms. Such a healthy church will produce healthy people filled with the attractiveness of Christ. This book aims to set each church free from confusion and ineffectiveness, so that each church can achieve the excellence God calls it to and reach as many as possible. It is this vision that fuels Richard Reising's passion, and it is this passion that makes *ChurchMarketing 101* worth reading and implementing."

Dr. Bill Lawrence, president, Leader Formation International

# ChurchMarketing 101

I am honored by God to have a wife who inspires and encourages me every step along the way. I dedicate this work to you, Michele, and to my family, my team, and to the many people who have stirred and challenged me forward in this adventurous Christian walk. I likewise dedicate this work to the church, which is ever sharpening its efforts to do more and reach more for the cause of Christ.

# Contents

# Introduction

What began as a vision written on tear-stained pages on a drafty bus in West Mexico has developed into a lifetime passion to see the body of Christ do more and reach more as our time approaches. God, as He has with all of us, set me up. He sent me to college initially as an engineering major, knowing that I would see no end there, and led me daily through a journey with a major detour into a marketing class. One day as I sat in class, my heart seemed to pound out of my chest. I knew almost instantly that this was what I was called to do—but it was years before I began to apprehend that for which He had apprehended me. From that point forward, I would spend years utilizing my marketing skills in the "real world" without ever envisioning their application in the church, despite having been in volunteer and part-time ministry since I was seventeen. Then, while on a missions trip in Mexico, I had a bus ride with God.

I knew that day my life had taken on a new direction. It was not an audible voice but rather the still small one that the Scripture reveals. After days of pursuing Him to resolve this life-changing feeling that had no definition, God poured into my heart a calling to teach the church about marketing. Out of nowhere, these words echoed in my heart. The church still promoted itself as if it was time-warped in the 1950s. It had in so many places lost its ability to connect with the outside world.

At the time, church marketing was hardly spoken of. I had never even thought about this colossal disconnection with the world before, but suddenly it was so clear. I was inspired and comforted as I began to recognize that the fundamentals of marketing strategy such as demographics, packaging, and basic psychology, which the corporate world relied on, were fully applicable to the church. Even more, many of the marketing strategies I had implemented were actually complementary to Scripture.

I began to recognize that churches were scratching their heads left and right, struggling for growth and not understanding what was creating shrinkage or sustained success. I sat in awe, challenged by the God of the universe to move forward in a dream, to build a team, and to shout a new passion from the rooftops.

I shared it with Michele, my then-girlfriend, now my wife, who interrupted me to say that God had given her a similar dream that very week. Six months later we married and were off to Arizona to follow God, who was taking us to the next step in a wild ride. I was offered a position as the marketing director of a high-tech firm, while Michele held the same position for an advertising agency, serving clients such as Nike and North Face.

We also served as youth pastors while I learned valuable lessons at the office and as a corporate marketing consultant on the side, lessons that I would need to know to serve the church—like how to build a boat while at sea, how to relate to and attract clients (like Intel and Motorola) without a comparable marketing budget, and how to leverage my knowledge of target markets to garner powerful results. I also learned a lot about what not to do. I learned how companies could shoot themselves in the foot by not evaluating external perspectives and not knowing what people really were looking for. I learned that marketing is much bigger than anyone thinks and that communication is not communication until it has been said a thousand times more than you think is necessary, and only then are you beginning to communicate.

After many years of consistently fulfilling the day job, we felt God move in us again. My wife and I were on a plane to Costa

Rica for a friend's wedding when we looked at each other and said, "It's time, isn't it!" It was time to launch out and begin the dream. We knew it was. I was excited—it was coming to pass.

I remember walking into my CEO's office to quit my job. My heart was racing with fear and excitement. Once he recognized there was nothing he could do to make me stay, he (a private investment banker with a jaded church experience) became so excited about what we were doing that he offered me $400,000 to help start this new venture. My heart had no peace with that. I turned down his generous offer and we left lives of executive salary to, in our first two years, qualify for welfare in the pursuit of this dream to which we had no map.

*ChurchMarketing 101* is a part of what God has revealed to us over the years as we have been honored to work with and inspire thousands of churches in almost every state and in more than a dozen countries. It is the fruit of campaigns that have shaped church culture and given broken churches a second chance. It represents the advice that made the growing church stronger and the megachurch more effective. It is born from the tears of pastors and from consulting with staffs of all shapes, sizes, ethnicities, and denominations. Yet, above all, it is the way God is calling His church to relate to a lost and dying world—the same way He challenged it over two thousand years ago; but somehow we have lost the way.

We have watched churches jump into the process of a contemporary marketing makeover, yet they still often sit floundering for real results. They have learned to send out mailers, they have followed leading churches and installed coffee bars, but they are still failing with the basic elements that create growth. New logos, new names, and new buildings by themselves do not inherently lead to new growth.

You cannot find the answer to growth for your church in mimicking what growing churches *do*—you are more likely to find it in what they *are*. Marketing is not a by-product of a department; it is the sense of self your church conveys on your members and your community. It is the destination port by which you navigate into the future. Calculating and delivering accurately with it can yield incredible results.

Interestingly, after all this time, I am still amazed at how much of what is being called marketing in the church is just "fluffery." Marketing is not simply about applying neat promotional ideas. Those are not the strategies I am talking about. It is so much deeper. Marketing is part of the infrastructure for growth. It is not the flashy paint on the outside—it is the steel beams that hold up the walls. That is why I have called this book *ChurchMarketing 101*. It is not 101 because it is simplified; it is 101 because it is fundamental.

For me, it is extremely important that you would know my heart as it relates to this topic. I will share much about managing perception, and I will challenge you to approach this topic with honor. If you think for a second that I am advocating manipulation or deceit, this is not the case. Marketing, to me, is not about sugarcoating or misrepresenting; it is about effectively communicating. It is meant to support a work that God is doing in your church—not to replace it.

Also, there is no suggestion here to compromise the gospel or suppress the ministry of God's Spirit. The presence of God and a strong scriptural foundation are prerequisites to any movement of God in our churches. The suggestions of this book assume that if you are reading this, you have a heart for sharing Christ with people and seeing your church grow. I will not get into divisive doctrinal issues but rather will attempt to help all churches focus on forming stronger connections and developing deeper bonds of relevancy with those whom they are trying to affect for God. The pursuit of this end largely removes our differences anyway. And please do not be hung up on the word *marketing*. Use the words *communications* or *connecting with people* in its place to help you if you must. And know—no one here is talking about "selling God." I am, however, very passionate about helping you put your best foot forward in representing Him to a lost world.

If I am successful, by the end of this book you will see marketing in a different light. You will have new ways to position your church for success. You will have a better sense of "self," a more vivid vision, and defined steps toward fulfilling what your church feels called to do.

The process will be engaging and challenging. At times, it might even be disheartening; but don't lose heart. Along the way you will be asked dozens of questions. Your answers will not provide a cookie-cutter solution, as there are none. They will, however, build upon each other and provide you with a personalized road map of change and growth.

I sincerely thank you for your willingness to see what marketing really is for the church—I pray you see new fruit born from its truths and find your God-given visions to be all the more within your grasp.

Chapter 1

The Premise • The Definition of Marketing • A Biblical Foundation for Marketing • A Biblical Charge for Marketing • Moving Forward

# What Is Church Marketing?

In 1996, I joined a high-tech firm to work for a VP of Marketing who had recently been hired away from one of the largest computer technology firms in the nation. God had already been stirring my heart with the vision of opening a ministry-focused marketing company to serve the body of Christ. At the time, I have to admit to wondering why He wasn't letting me start it then—I was wondering why He had prompted my wife and me to move across the country to take this position.

I began to learn "why" very quickly. I arrived on the heels of a promotional campaign launching a new production facility in the Silicon Valley. The executive team had orchestrated an enormous promotional campaign focused on bringing hundreds of industry professionals to see our incredible facilities and equipment for processing microchips. The promotions were seemingly successful, the responses were many, and our company, for a brief moment, considered the result a total victory.

That is, until months went by and we realized that no business had come from the entire promotion. The sales staff was frantic as the production team and a luxurious facility sat idle from lack of work. Costs were mounting into the millions. How could a campaign that looked so successful yield such dramatic, long-term failure? Here is what I learned.

I learned that when our sales team had paraded prospects through the facilities, the spotless, state-of-the-art machines sat idle. The production staff literally sat there without a thing to do while potential clients visited and evaluated the machines as they did our company. And the prospects simply wondered, "Why is no one working and why are the machines idle?" Because our staff did not help them think any other way, the prospects ultimately surmised, "It looks like no one else is willing to trust them with their microchips. Why should we?" Wow. Blistering. The team had never thought to run simulations or to fill the empty racks in the warehouse. They just kept showing prospect after prospect the nice equipment but no proof of knowledge or experience to warrant trusting the company with millions of dollars worth of their microchips.

I know it is easy now to see the mistake, but remember, these were million-dollar minds at work here. Yet no one stopped to think about what was being communicated to the people who had proven their interest in our company by coming to the launch. I mean, after all, they came, didn't they? Needless to say, I spent three and a half years with that firm trying to help clean up the hideous perceptions that were created simply because no one thought it through. In a service industry, machines and a nice facility do not give people confidence in you. Proving your ability to perform successfully for them and for others, however, makes all the difference.

You see, marketing is much more than promoting things. Marketing requires thinking it through. It involves every entity and interaction that fosters the outside world's perception of your organization. When you do not pay your bills, you're marketing. When you do not cut the grass, you're marketing. When you talk over the heads of your "prospects" or fail to serve them, you're marketing. You are shaping perception in the hearts and minds of your members and your target community—that is the very definition of marketing.

> When you do not pay your bills, you're marketing.
> When you do not cut the grass, you're marketing.

The factory launch debacle showed me what often happens in churches. Congregants are pushed to invite others to come and do so, out of love or duty, laying their reputations on the line with visitors. We, as the church, often do a poor job connecting with the people they bring—leaving visitors with an experience they do not value enough to return to. This leaves the inviter frustrated about the lost opportunity that many times had been so hard fought. We connect well with the "lifers," but do we connect with anyone else? This is a marketing issue.

This and many other great experiences were insights that God walked us through long before we ever took a stab at serving the body. Why? Because God is not as interested in promotion as He is in preparation. He is more concerned that you have created an environment to retain those who visit your church than He is that you compel them to come in. After all, when you have not prepared yourself, you do a poor job of representing Him. And although He is gloriously omnipotent, He is often shortchanged by our ability to connect with the outside world.

We often say in our seminars that over 50 percent of the churches in the United States *should not* promote themselves. Shocked? The simple reason is that if your congregants are not actively inviting people to your church, there are reasons why. If visitors are not staying, there are reasons why. What's even worse, by promoting a church that is not experiencing this internal success, some churches are damaging their ability for future growth. All they are doing is inviting the outside world in to see why no one wants to invite people to their church. These visitors attend once, never to return, and tell all their friends why they shouldn't bother trying that church. This creates the "buzz" or community perception of the church.

> If your congregants are not actively inviting people to your church, there are reasons why. If your visitors are not staying, there are reasons why.

This might be a hard saying, but have hope—there are solutions. This book deals with the heart of marketing—what I call premarketing—and that is the foundation of this book. Its purpose is to help those of you (pastors, elders, staff, leaders, and helpers of any sort) who can make a difference work together to create the place that truly connects people to Christ, fulfilling your calling as a church to perform the ministry of reconciliation (2 Cor. 5:19).

Most churches fail at marketing because they do not grasp that it encompasses every aspect of church life. They assume it is about things like passing out flyers, but it is much greater than that. True marketing is such a large concept that even those churches that say marketing has no place in the church simply do not realize that they are, in fact, currently doing it. In most cases, they are just doing it poorly. There is no church in the world that does not participate in marketing; there are just those that do it well and those that do not. After all, at the very core of marketing is the connection of people to an entity—and there are no entities more worthy of time, money, and effort than the body of Christ and Christ Himself.

## The Definition of Marketing

The concept of marketing spawns great praise and great criticism, yet almost all opinions are born of completely different definitions. The corporate world varies on what exactly marketing is, and the church world is even less enlightened.

Some assume marketing is sending out direct mail pieces or placing door hangers throughout the neighborhood. Others assume it finds its root in the same vein as telemarketing, and therefore think it is always intrusive. In reality, marketing deals on less superficial levels than we think.

If you take a college marketing class, you will undoubtedly be taught about the Four P's: "product" (what you are selling and its components/packaging, etc.), "place" (where it is distributed and by whom), "price" (what it costs—both to the seller and the buyer), and "promotion" (the tools you use to make it known).

Thus, in the church world, product is the gospel and the subsequent style, quality, relevance, and packaging. Place reflects your location, be it the church building, a small group, or a soapbox; it is the logistics of how you connect with your membership and the community. Price is harder to define. While Christ calls us to give everything, we have to realize that different churches communicate different costs—many churches grow by decreasing the cost of commitment, while others' costs are so high, the churches barely show any growth for years because they require so much, so fast. Promotion entails witnessing, public relations, advertising, and everything done to advance the church and the message.

You can see that the academic definition of marketing is large in scope. It affects your church's pulpit message and street address, business cards, altar call, building signage, and much, much more. These are all textbook attributes of your current marketing effort.

Let's look at another definition of marketing. Merriam-Webster says that marketing is "an aggregate (sum) of functions involved in moving goods from producer to consumer."

Interesting. It incorporates much more than door hangers. It is "the sum" of all your church does to connect Christ with your membership and the outside world. It is "the sum" of things that are done (including all that defines your product, place, etc.) to engage someone to respond positively to the very thing you are promoting. These things or functions all combine to establish one central reality in the person or persons you are pursuing—that reality being their perception of your church and what it has to offer. All your church has done and does, including your members and your denomination, combines to shape what people think—and ultimately forms their thoughts on whether they consider your church. Sound heavy? There is often much to overcome, thus the need to communicate so clearly and so deliberately with those you are trying to reach—because you often only get one chance. The old saying "You never get a second chance to make a first impression" holds very true here.

True marketing is a lot to take in. In fact, we spent years toiling with this vague definition, struggling to see how to communicate the power of marketing to churches, when God simply put together the best definition we have seen to date. It encompasses all the standard definitions and is packaged in a way that empowers you to easily evaluate your church's marketing efforts on every level—at every point of contact with people.

*Marketing is the management of perception.* That's it. Plain and simple. Marketing. Managing people's perceptions toward the hopeful end that they will respond to Christ and His church.

As a church or an organization, marketing is the ability to adjust and control how people perceive you by helping define their connection with you and affecting their decisions toward Christ and your church. Under the umbrella of marketing are such topics and efforts as ministry style, building aesthetics, advertising, signage, handling visitors, ushering, welcoming, announcements, church name, location, communication, and much more.

And please note, managing perception is not about manipulating the truth, it is about effectively presenting reality. You have to first become the message you communicate.

To take full advantage of this definition, let's define *perception*. Perception is how people feel about a thing. It is how they see a thing in relationship to themselves and to other things from their mindshare. When I say, "Tabasco," you think "hot" (unless you are from Louisiana, then you might think "cologne"). You have a place for it in your mental file between "bell peppers" and "raw jalapeños." Now, if I say, "Baptist," or "Church of Christ," where do you file those? In what categories do they fit within your mind? People's perception is so powerful that it is commonly understood that "perception is reality" and it is literally "real" to those whose experiences have formed their perceptions. Do people perceive your church as boring? Exciting? Weird? Plain? Stuffy? Lower class? Upper class? Don't know how they perceive you? Don't worry, we'll talk about how to know. Don't think you can change those perceptions? You can. It's called marketing. Marketing strategy founded in truth gives you the wings to shape perception. For some, you might actually have to make changes in your church in order to change what people think of your church—and you might have to overcompensate for your history.

If marketing is the management of perception, what is the definition of management? Management is simply the ability to know where you are today, to know where you would like to be in the future, and to make adjustments along the way. Thus, if I have a good manager in my company, I have someone who is (1) on top of things today, (2) in line with his or her goals for tomorrow, and (3) analyzing and adjusting as needed to stay the course. A manager like that is priceless! How's that for Management 101?

Let's put this all back together to foster a greater understanding of marketing. Marketing is the management of perception, and management is knowing where you stand today, where your goals lie tomorrow, and making adjustments. Therefore, at the very core of marketing is (1) the ability to understand how people perceive you today; (2) to have a vision for how you would like them to perceive you (within their own frame of reference); and (3) to make decisive strides and adjustments in your way of doing and communicating things to ensure that people ultimately learn to perceive you as you desire.

That's it. But you must start with the ability to establish two things: (1) how people (your members and your community) think about your church (or if they do at all), and (2) what your clearly defined goal is for how you want them to think about you—based in reality. How do you want to differentiate yourself from other churches? How do you uniquely meet the specific needs of your community? What type of people are most at home in the church you have—what type fit best in the church you want to be?

To be truly effective and upright, communication has to be wrought out of truth—it has to be consistent with who you are

> Marketing must first affect who we become before it can affect those we pursue.

as a church. This means if you communicate that you are the church "where love is," love had better be there in abundance. It had better be flowing out the doors, or you are using false advertising and you will pay for that the hard way. Marketing must first affect who we become before it can affect those we pursue. If it does not, we promote hypocrisy and drive people even farther away.

Marketing is the management of perception. Wonder if this concept is biblically based? Keep reading.

## A Biblical Foundation for Marketing

Do you wonder where God stands on marketing? If we understand the premise that marketing is the management of perception, we will see God's Word unfold with a brilliant new light, as we understand how He worked in lives thousands of years ago to manage perceptions, just as He does today. Two thousand years ago He did it through Christ—today He works through His body.

> There are over thirty references to Jesus perceiving people's perception and changing His ministry direction, re-communicating, or deciding to halt communications altogether.

Think about it—how many times do you remember the Scriptures saying, "Jesus perceived their thoughts, and said . . ."? There are over thirty references to Jesus perceiving people's perception and changing His ministry direction, re-communicating, or deciding to halt communications altogether. Wow, Jesus perceived (marketing word, remember?) their perception (thoughts) of Him, and He said or did specific things to change the way people perceived Him. What Jesus did in His own ministry falls beautifully into our clarified definition of marketing. After feeding the five thousand, Jesus traveled to Magdala. The disciples, joining him there, had forgotten to bring bread with them. In Matthew 16:8–9, the Bible says:

But Jesus, being aware of it, said to them, "O you of little faith, why do you reason among yourselves because you have brought no bread? Do you not yet understand, or remember the five loaves of the five thousand and how many baskets you took up?"

Jesus managed perception. The perception was that Jesus was limited because of something His disciples had done. He wanted them to know that He is more than able. His communication reminded them of His past miracles. Sounds like simple communication, right? It is. Remember, that is the foundation of marketing—know how people perceive you, know how you want them to perceive you, and communicate in such a way that it shapes the way they think about you or your product.

Jesus relevantly shaped communication to the ears of the person He was attempting to reach. Not unlike Peter, who on the day of Pentecost "perceived" that the crowd thought they were drunk after the Holy Spirit had moved upon them. Peter's marketing effort: "These men are not drunk, as you suppose. It's only nine in the morning! No, this is what was spoken by the prophet Joel" (Acts 2:15–16 NIV). Peter understood where the crowd was coming from. He felt it important that the crowd also understand that what they were seeing was not lunacy but Scripture revealed in daily life. He knew what he wanted people to think and shaped the communication of the "service" to give people the proper perspective. Good marketing.

Now, you might be bothered by my use of the term *marketing* in relation to Scripture, but there is no arguing that Jesus and Peter and many others throughout Scripture concerned themselves with what others perceived, and pursued relevant or relatable communications as a means to a positive end. They actively sought to influence and change the perceptions of their listeners. In fact, most people who argue against marketing are simply caught up in a semantics issue. They see marketing as some commercial transaction, where, in reality, it is merely the act of shaping perception. If I convince you of something, wouldn't you say that you "bought in" to my idea? Of course, you bought it. It was a transaction that became more palatable the more I communicated things that connected you to the idea or product. In this case, it is beyond a product. It is the God of the universe, and He works through His Spirit to speak to people through His body—the church (Rom. 10:14). He also has a third-party salesperson that assists—the Holy Spirit—and He works in lives to woo people to Christ. That means we have help! So, let's let go of the misconceptions over the wording and catch the principle here.

Jesus even did certain things (marketing efforts—created to shape perception) just to help people understand Him better. Do you remember when Lazarus died and Jesus went to his tomb to pray? "So they took away the stone. Then Jesus looked up and said, 'Father, I thank you that you have heard me. I knew that you always hear me, *but I said this for the benefit of the people standing here, that they may believe that you sent me'*" (John 11:41–42 NIV, emphasis mine). Jesus actually prayed a prayer that He deemed unnecessary to pray except for the fact it helped people perceive and better understand the nature of who He was and what He was doing. The purpose of that prayer was to help people understand, more than it was to move the hand of God.

How about this one? You think my comment that more than 50 percent of churches should not promote themselves is ridiculous? Think it is crazy for a church not to want to promote itself for a season? Even Jesus knew that self-promotion was sometimes a bad idea. In the book of Mark, on more than ten occasions, Jesus told people whom He had healed not to tell anyone about what happened. Sometimes, the timing is just not right for publicity—it is important to know the season you are in (a subject we'll get to soon).

Think about it. Jesus was always communicating in such a way as to provoke the desired reaction—because He knew deep down what the people needed to hear. In fact, you'll recall that

Jesus spoke very differently to different groups of people. When did you see Him lash out at a sinner? Never. You heard Him slam the hypocritical religious leaders, though. You read that He loved the sinner, taught parables to the seeker, and gave what, at the time, were harsh lifestyle challenges to His disciples. In each case, He was cognizant of people's perceptions of Him, and He ministered to people according to where they were in life. He marketed His message so appropriately that He affected people right where they lived. He communicated grace to the sinner, His Word to the hungry, His challenges to the committed, and His unabated truth to the hardened of heart. Jesus ministered on all levels. Are we?

> Jesus communicated grace to the sinner, His Word to the hungry, His challenges to the committed, and His unabated truth to the hardened of heart. Jesus ministered on all levels. Are we?

It is clear that in some of these cases, Jesus's recognition of others' perceptions was an act of divine insight. We will have to work a bit harder to understand where people are coming from in some instances. But can we not still reason and perceive? Can't we follow Christ's example and attempt to shape perception by our communication—including our websites, printed materials, sermons, or signage? Can't we understand that people who walk through our church doors come from all categories of life? Connecting with them stems from communicating God's truth on their level in a way that will shape perception of not only your church but of a loving God who has tried so desperately to connect with them.

## A Biblical Charge for Marketing

Christ's Great Commission is marketing in its most traditional sense. He said, "Go into all the world and preach the gospel to every creature" (Mark 16:15). The word *preach* indicates that we are to announce, publish, make known, and proclaim the gospel. Its very definition indicates one of the pillars of marketing—*promotion*. Promotion goes hand in hand with the Great Commission. Jesus even coupled the commission with "signs" that follow. He indicated His desire to demonstrate His Word in an effort to validate and reinforce perception.

Our challenge as the New Testament church is a marketing one. It is to help the world perceive Christ not for who we have been but for who He is. Even His commandment to love one another was to affect the perception of the masses. "By this all will know that you are My disciples, if you have love for one another" (John 13:35). God is very interested in how we represent Him. That is why Jesus pulled the disciples aside and gave them such hard sayings. As judgment always starts in the house of God (1 Peter 4:17), is it not because God understands that our behavior so strongly affects the world's perception of Him? So let's change the way the world looks at Christians. Let's shape their perception by embracing His Spirit and connecting with people at the level they live.

Other charges have been given to us as well. One of my personal favorites is from Paul as he wrote in 1 Corinthians 9:19–23:

> For though I am free from all men, I have made myself a servant to all, that I might win the more; and to the Jews I became as a Jew, that I might win Jews; to those who are under the law, as under the law, that I might win those who are under the law; to those who are without law, as without law (not being without law toward God, but under law toward Christ), that I might win those who are without law; to the weak I became as weak, that I might win the weak. I have become all things to all men, that I might by all means save some. Now this I do for the gospel's sake, that I may be partaker of it with you.

Marketing's foundation is found in the context of whom you are trying to reach. Paul knew that his success in ministry was proportional to how relevant he was to those he attempted to persuade. His ability to manage their perception began with knowing that different people come from completely different directions and that to "win one" he had to endeavor to become as "one"—he even indicates that he "is made all things"—showing us that it is God who is performing the action on a yielded vessel. Yielding to relevance for the gospel's sake is an act of devotion.

Now, Paul would not suggest that you should become a cannibal to win a cannibal, but he certainly would pursue the knowledge of how they "perceived" things, in the pursuit of establishing Jesus as Lord in their hearts and minds.

Where does that leave us? It leaves us commissioned to promote the gospel (by Jesus) and challenged to do market research (by Paul) and shown the way to communicate differently to different people by both. It is incumbent upon us to take up the cross, deny ourselves, and live a life worthy of Christ—passionately and relevantly marketing or representing Him well in everything we do. After all, God says Himself in 1 Samuel 16:7 that the nature of man is to look on the outward appearance. As much as we know God is a God of the heart, we have to acknowledge that those with un-renewed minds make decisions based on the outside, before God begins to clean them on the inside.

Therefore, as individual churches, it is your challenge to reach people where they are and to create the atmosphere of love and joy that people hunger for. Your challenge is to relate to people wherever they might be in life and to relevantly connect them to Christ and His kingdom.

### Moving Forward

We have spent the last chapter in a very "academic" (boring) mode, which is not my style at all. But, just as you build a house on a steady foundation, marketing the church is the same. If you feel you already have this foundation down and are wondering when the pace will pick up, I challenge you to stay the course. Consider chapters 1 and 2 to be *base camp*. Hang with me through these chapters. In chapters 3 and 4, we begin a wild ride of *exploration*—finding hidden keys of insight into your community and your church. In chapters 5 and 6, we focus on *preparation*—calibrating what you already do to garner significant growth results. In 7 and 8, we uncover powerful *strategic application*—setting your church apart with deliberate intent. In chapters 9 and 10, we will launch out into *visionary pursuit*, which will change everything. Each chapter builds upon the previous one and creates a momentum that can change the life of your church and impact your community for eternity.

At the end of each chapter I will challenge you as pastors, leaders, and church workers to reflect and to jot down your thoughts. Remember to keep track of your writings. They will culminate in a framework for your marketing efforts—for understanding where you are, where you are called to be, and what changes you will need to make.

Marketing might not be what you thought it was. Many who have not seen it as you and I have still think marketing is solely about promotions. We know it is about so much more. It is about perception management. All over corporate America marketing departments and marketing firms are working relentlessly to analyze how companies are perceived and calculating how to reposition them. They consider such elements as product, place, price, and promotion and utilize tools such as marketing research, demographics, focus groups, advertising, promotions, and public relations to adjust perception.

In the church, we take this understanding and see that not only is the concept biblical but that, just as in Christ's day, overcoming misperceptions and connecting people with the truth is a holy charge—fundamental to the Christian cause. When the perceptions we aim to create are godly and based on reality, we can communicate from a backbone of truth. When they are based on a false reality, perception management becomes deception—a line none of us wants to cross.

We determined marketing comes from (1) knowing how people perceive your church today; (2) having a vision for how you would like them to perceive you (within their own frame of reference); and (3) making decisive strides and adjustments in your way of doing and communicating things, from promotion to pulpits, to ensure that people ultimately perceive you as you desire.

Take a moment to consider. What do the people in your community think about your church? What do different types of people in your church think about your church? What do you want them to think? What are you doing right now to change that? What will you have to do to make a real difference in how people see you? Take some time and write down your thoughts. Remember, there are no cookie-cutter solutions. Your answers will help you know who you are as a church and will build upon each other as we go along to create a bridge to the church you are called to be.

Chapter 2

Where Perception Comes From • Reading between the Lines • Church Marketing Gone Wrong • Stumbling Blocks and Building Blocks • Moving Forward

# How Marketing Affects Every Area of Your Church

A marketing professor holds an item up in the air. He asks the class, "What is this item worth?" Students chime in suggesting one dollar, ten dollars, three hundred, and more. After much deliberation, the professor simply says, "Well, you are all wrong." He watches the class wax frustrated as he finally reveals, "The item is worth whatever someone will pay me for it." He goes on to explain that this is universally true.

We see this all the time, don't we? You've probably heard someone say, "All you're paying for in that product is the name." A higher priced car, stereo, set of golf clubs, purse, or cosmetics—we all try to justify these expensive purchases, but many times we are buying a name or a style. Sometimes the product is truly different and legitimately more valuable. Sometimes it is just packaging that sells us—sometimes it is a sense of belonging.

Have you ever looked at the shampoo aisle in the grocery store? What is the difference between the $2 bottle and the $24 bottle? You'll often find the exact same ingredients. Ask yourself, "If two cars are the same, but one carries a Mercedes emblem, would I pay more for it?" A small difference in any one thing can make a large difference in how something is perceived.

I read a story about a finance consultant who held a seminar in which he charged $95 per person. He had fewer than ten people show up. Frustrated, he tried a different approach. He took his seminar to another city and this time charged $995. Over three hundred people came. The difference? Although the content was the same, people expected to receive more from a $995 seminar than they did from a $95 one.

## Where Perception Comes From

So many things play a part in our perception. Colors can connote such things as comfort, affluence, cheapness, joy, and belonging. Structure can convey openness, stuffiness, a sense of welcoming, and status. We cannot pretend the small things do not affect how people see our churches. We have to realize that perception is framed from two major components: (1) what people see and hear about us, and (2) where they are in life.

Let's think about the main components that make up our churches' marketing efforts, the main areas that contribute to how we are perceived. To start, we should always focus on whom we are trying to reach and the ways we create their perception of us. I pray this overview will stir your heart and mind and enable you to see your church accurately in your own eyes, the eyes of your congregation and community, and through prayer, in the eyes of God.

Why?

So you can make adjustments and prepare to boldly promote it—knowing that you are right on target with the people you are uniquely called to reach, and knowing that you have maximized the internal church experience to ensure that, when they come, they will have the opportunity to come face-to-face with God's love, unhampered by distractions that the "faithful" have learned to overlook. Let's always keep in mind that the nature of man is to look and judge first on outward appearances (1 Sam. 16:7). Thus, unchurched people cannot be expected to understand the intents of our hearts from the outset.

One of my favorite marketing illustrations goes like this: "A woman is driving down a lonely, pitch-dark road late at night and sees that she is almost out of gas. Her fear is somewhat relieved as she sees two gas stations up ahead. If these two gas stations are equally accessible and the gas is equally priced, which will she choose?" Plain and simple. She will choose the one with the better lighting. Why? At that moment, her primary need is safety. Better lighting makes her feel safer. Her response is natural and just as natural as the first conclusions that people commonly draw about churches.

Think about this story as it relates to your church. Why would someone choose to visit? What is it about you that would make them think that you have the answer and you would welcome them in? What sets your church apart?

When we wonder what people in our communities might think of us, it is almost unnerving to consider all the points of contact those conclusions can be drawn from. The perception that people have of any church can be based on something as simple as your church's drive-by curb appeal. It can also be based completely on assumptions, on what has been learned from others, solely from your website, or even on denominational stereotypes.

Let's first focus on those things we can control: areas of church life where we often don't connect well with the unchurched world. What you will see is that the efforts of marketing are church-wide. While they ultimately require the championing skills of the church leadership, they also rest on the shoulders of ushers, teachers, children's ministry workers, greeters, and everyone who makes contact on behalf of the church.

Following is a sample of the elements that can form someone's perceptions of your church, either experienced firsthand or through the media, friends, and other secondhand sources:

- The concept of church in general
- The denomination of your church (or lack thereof)
- Specific elements of your church:
  Church name
  Curb appeal
  External promotion
  Location
  Website
  Worship style
  Ministry style
  Ministry focus

Vocabulary

Signage

Décor

Attire of the leadership or members

The types and number of cars in the parking lot

Doctrine

History of your church

Printed materials

Leadership team

Greeters

Children's ministry

Youth ministry

The pastor/minister

Current members

Past members

What people from other churches say about your church

And hundreds more . . .

You can see that church marketing is a team effort. Pastors or ministers cannot do this alone. If they are forced to embody or carry the weight of this marketing obligation, a church will likely suffer dramatically in their absence. Have you ever seen a church suffer a drop in attendance in the absence of its primary leader? It is often because the attractive teaching style or ministry spirit has never been trained or imparted to the leadership or the congregation as a whole. It becomes all about "the man." On the flip side, what if you had a clearly defined marketing (perception management) effort, championed by the leadership team and embraced by the staff and volunteers as the benchmark for policies and communication? Wouldn't you have the ability to shape church culture to purposefully affect lives in a clear and powerful way?

## Reading between the Lines

Similar to being in a play, everyone in the church has a role that is part of the experience a visitor takes away. If your visitors feel encouraged, or snubbed, or welcomed, or loved, or mistreated, those impressions come from their contextualized experience. They place everything they see at your church into a context that fits with their predispositions. In the last chapter we talked about some of the specific things that form someone's perception. Now, let's look at how those elements shape someone's idea of who we are—how people "read between the lines" to draw conclusions from various impressions they receive. While you read this, think about what you might be telling your community. After all, you are living epistles, "known and read by all men" (2 Cor. 3:2).

Let's start with roughly the same list we used on the previous pages. Each of these elements plays a specific role in framing how an outsider defines your church.

### Concept of Church in General

This is one you likely have the least influence over in the beginning. It is the psychological imprint outsiders have developed over time. Church might draw out feelings of guilt, nostalgia, triviality, or the ever-common thought, "church people are all hypocrites." Whatever their initial feeling, much of what outsiders think is the result of the remarks of others or past experiences with church and churchgoers.

### Denomination or Lack Thereof

Many people have, at the least, a vague sense of what a particular denomination stands for or at least a grasp of common stereotypes connected with the denomination. Think about a number of denominations in your own mind. See how the mental pictures are based on what you know and what you have heard about doctrinal and lifestyle tendencies associated with each one? Chances are, even nonchurch people have a general sense of what those differences are. Throughout different parts of the country, people tend to have common regional perceptions of each denomination. So go ahead and face it. You are going to have to deal with this. Your visitors may think they know you by your denominational title. What if your church's denomination is considered less "popular" than others in your community? That will add to your challenge of making a visitor's experience at your church a positive one. Unfamiliarity with your particular denomination can make your church seem "fringe" to an outsider. It may make people say condescendingly, "I wonder what that's all about." Being unknown is not enticing to outsiders in the church world; it is disconcerting.

Your church does not escape this issue if it does not have a denomination. Nondenominational is still a common category. The challenge is that it spreads a wide variety of views. You might even become lumped in with other churches that have very dissimilar styles and doctrines from yours.

In considering the impact of denomination in an outsider's snap categorization, it is important to know that in many parts of the country there exists even deeper passion about denominations. In some cases, the reaction may be so adverse that potential visitors may actively and vigorously reject your denomination and swear to avoid it even though they have never heard your heart or stepped foot in your church. These rivers often run deep.

### Church Name

Names of churches have a number of origins. Some have stood the test of centuries while others change annually. Some are derived from biblical reflection. Some reflect the specific passions of the church, while others are designed specifically to create a bridge to the unchurched. Whatever its origin, no matter how long it has been in use, the name of a church says a lot to a visitor. It can evoke feelings of inclusion or exclusion. It can make the church seem prestigious, divisive, or playful. It can flow beautifully off the tip of your tongue or be a mouthful that requires explanation. It might say too little or too much about what you could be. It can give connotations of economic status, ethnicity, social standing, and even indicate a sense of the required commitment level. A name says a lot.

I'll never forget the time a church client asked for help in designing a children's logo. The name of the ministry was "Hands On Kids' Ministry." Without proper pause, this name alone could make a parent turn and about-face. To make matters worse, the client wanted the logo to be handprints laid over images of children. Their intent was pure—attempting to reinforce that the ministry was hands-on—but the connotation could have been taken quite negatively.

### Curb Appeal

This is your opportunity to attract people who do not go to church. It is how you roll out the red carpet, so to speak. The more appealing the church is to a visitor based on a perception of how the church matches the person's lifestyle, the more likely visitors will put that one high on their list when looking for a church. It also conveys, without words, a number of things about your church's priorities, social connections, and financial status. The attention you pay to the appearance of the church grounds and the exterior of the building transmits unmistakable messages. Are your church grounds so ill-kept that the unchurched might be ashamed to be seen entering the church? Or, at the other extreme, does the attention to your church's physical appearance keep it so well maintained that you intimidate and convey only pomp and affluence?

### External Promotion

One of the marketing methods that churches have caught on to in the last decade is external promotion. External promotion gets the word out about your church. As more and more churches use direct mail, billboards, Yellow Pages, newspapers, movie theaters, and the like, the allure of being "the church that advertises" decreases because so many are doing it. What remains is an opportunity to differentiate yourself in the recipients' minds from any number of churches that are vying for people's mindshare. This is your chance to open the doors of your church and give people a glimpse of what is inside. It is often where a church lets its personality (or lack thereof) out of the bag. There are certain immediately identifiable factors that come across: tone, design style, ability to communicate effectively to the unchurched, a sense of values, and even a glimpse into lifestyle categories. It is important to remember that repetition (both in continued promotion and in consistency of design and communication style) breeds a coherent sense of self. Sporadic promotion is like saying "hello" once, where continued promotion is like dropping by to say "hello" on a regular basis. Which approach would make you feel most comfortable when making a church decision? Efforts with consistency simply pay off.

Promotion is a valid opportunity to extend your curb appeal to someone's doorstep. Of course, this assumes you have savvy to connect from a design and communication standpoint. Many efforts fall short, simply reinforcing how disconnected the church is. This is a media-saturated world, and people are communicated to professionally on a continual basis. Unprofessional communication stands out as such. To ensure you connect, promotion needs to be drawn on a line between who you are as a church and the values and styles represented by your target audience. What appeals to them?

### Location

You know the catchphrase "Location is everything" or "Location. Location. Location." Location is fundamental to the success of retail stores and restaurants. It is factored into the value of your home. Location is more than just about the drive time getting there. Location means instant classification in terms of your immediate surroundings.

Of course, location is important. It is not, however, "everything." Even Jesus challenged and overcame geographical prejudices. "And Nathanael said to him [regarding Jesus], 'Can anything good come out of Nazareth?' Philip said to him, 'Come and see'" (John 1:46). Have you objectively considered the pros and cons of your church's location? Unless you can move the church, you might have challenges to overcome through your marketing.

### Types and Number of Cars in the Parking Lot

This speaks volumes; it can tell an outsider what type of people attend your church, what they value, and even in a general sense, how they are doing financially. It also serves as a quick gauge of the present demand for your church. A big parking lot with just a few cars conveys a lot to the outside world about the demand for what you are offering.

### Website

Your website is an extension of your external promotion. It is fair to say that if someone is looking for a church in your area, they will, in most places, search the Internet. In doing so, they will search for what is important to them, be it denomination, children's programs, or overall offerings. People will likely review six to twelve websites before making a decision. Internet presence has become the primary way people evaluate churches—meaning, of the ten websites they looked at, they evaluated all ten, even though they visited only one church. As a result, just how important is it that your website connects? Does it roll out the red carpet? Is the navigation built with visitors in mind, or is it apparent to them that they are on the outside looking in? Is it up to date or is your Christmas program still being advertised in March? Does it put your best face out there? Does it give potential visitors a glimpse of life inside of your church and break down the barriers to a comfortable visit? Will they feel like they already know you and that you are "their kind of people"?

Please commit this to memory: websites are seldom read, but they are always evaluated. What you are showing them is communicating on a level high above the word-for-word details of your site. You are communicating so much about your lifestyle as a church. As a matter of fact, the website visit is the closest thing to being in your church a visitor is likely to experience. If your website is effective, it will create a bridge to a visit by giving people visual clues that you have common lifestyles and values. In other words, this is where they will learn if they "fit" in your church. Remember, people are likely to look at ten or so church websites; they will attend the one or two churches that connect with them the best. If your website is good enough to get those "votes," it might even be good enough to score in another important category: being attractive enough for your members to want to share the website with their friends as an introduction to their church.

> Websites are seldom read, but they are always evaluated.

### Greeters, Ushers, and Leadership Team Members

People who stand out as official representatives of a church serve as an immediate indicator for visitors. How a greeter treats them is a huge factor in determining what their future relationship with the church will be. After all, the visitor knows what this person is there for and what to expect. Every opportunity for a handshake and a smile sets the tone for the visit. Every missed chance diminishes the potential to truly reach that visitor. In addition, the age, ethnicity, and attire of these leaders helps visitors determine if this is "their kind of church." It is a truism that you "never get a second chance to make a first impression." Who is making the first impression for your church, and is that impression the one you want?

### Signage

Signage tells visitors how important they are to the church. The lack of clear directions can be an indicator that making them feel welcome is an afterthought. It can also make them feel they are left out of the "know" on purpose. The age and quality of the signage also says a lot.

Take a look around your church. Would I know where visitor parking is? Would I know where the main entrance is? Would I know where the services are held? Could I find the restrooms without asking? If I had children, would I know where to take them without making myself obviously out of place? Whom would I ask if I had questions?

### Logo

Some logos are literal; they say what they mean and mean what they say. Others are figurative, conveying an emotion or tone. What your church logo says to your congregation can be very different than what it says to the outside world. We love what the cross represents; visitors may have only a vague idea of what it means. Some logos make us feel better about ourselves. Some can make outsiders feel more optimistic about themselves. Logos can be positive, negative, or just there. Their frequency and consistency of use conveys a deeper sense that the church knows itself well.

I recently spoke with a church that was dealing with a logo problem. Their logo was complex and wildly colorful. It meant a lot to the pastor. It was a visual representation of a message he had felt particularly stirred about. The logo made great sense after you heard the message, and the pastor loved how he could refer to it quickly to get the whole team to remember the points of the message at any time. The challenge is that it took a forty-five minute sermon to understand.

The logo worked well internally but caused confusion to those outside the church. Confusion is never good. If people do not understand your communication to them, they will assume you are not trying to communicate to them—you are in your own world. When you are considering a big decision like a logo, ask yourself, What is the purpose of a logo? You might have varied answers, but I would challenge that it is to identify and distinguish yourself in your community more than it is to tell a story or to cheer on the believers. If you need a logo to remind members of what your church is all about, I suggest there is a breakdown in communication somewhere else.

### Worship Style

As believers, we have a plethora of different styles of worship, and most of us have relatively strong preferences as to what we like and don't like. We cannot expect the unchurched to recognize what is "good" or "bad" by our standards. There will be, however, a number of things we know they will recognize and respond to in their own way: audience participation in singing, variance from what they perceive to be "normal church music," quality of vocal and instrumental composition, and in a general overall sense—whether it was "boring," "uplifting," "melancholy," or "dramatic."

I have been in services where I fell asleep during worship, and I have been in one where I saw a lady cut a cartwheel (no exaggeration!). I have heard full choirs sing without a leader, and

I have seen a music minister who performed like Neil Diamond. Different strokes for different folks holds somewhat true, but something is generally a concern if visitors can feel that what they witnessed was extreme—either on the bizarre side or the emotionless side.

### Ministry Style and Focus

Unless they are actively involved in searching for a church, your visitors are not likely to have the context to understand how good your ministry might be compared to other churches. What they will certainly notice is if it is down-to-earth or delivered in "preacher tone." Does it relate to topics they understand and are dealing with right now in life, or is it focused on the esoteric and academic? Is it harsh, soft, bold, or weak? These are things they can pick up on. Style (tone) is something people universally pick up; topic focus (relevance) is relational.

### Vocabulary

Visitors cannot be expected to know everything. The one thing they do know is what they don't know. When they hear words they don't recognize, one of two things usually happens. If they are taught what these words mean, they will feel included in the conversation. If the words are not explained, visitors will be confused by the usage and made to feel excluded and unimportant.

We all develop verbal shortcuts among groups we are involved in. They not only save time, they reinforce our sense of community and belonging. Unfortunately, those shortcuts also build walls between us and outsiders. Think about your church's vocabulary. Do you need a degree in theology to understand it? How many times do you use words that non-churchgoers cannot comprehend without proper explanation? Consider this: almost all nonbelievers are unable to accurately define a word as common to us as *grace*.

I'll never forget a specific direct mail piece that a church asked us to design for them. The piece was to be targeted specifically to nonchurch people, and the slogan was to be "Jubilee Celebration—Come Experience the Anointing." Small problem: nonchurch people would have no idea what *jubilee* is and even less idea what *anointing* is. Talk about setting the wrong foot forward. In this situation, a whole community would have felt alienated from the church without even stepping foot inside.

### Décor

Décor sets a tone. It might be warm or cool. It might be traditional, contemporary, or worse, historic contemporary (based on an attempt to be contemporary years ago and now style has passed you by). Décor can be conservative, traditional, fanciful, or extravagant; it says volumes about your church culture.

Here's a word of caution. If your church culture is overly expressive, reinforcing that with extravagant décor will likely push you past the edge of normalcy in most people's book. If your church atmosphere is notably mundane, décor to match your mood will make your church feel like a mausoleum. If you have a church style that is off what your community sees as dead center, use your décor to counterbalance it, not to reinforce it.

### Printed Materials

Like a website, it is fair to say of brochures and the like that they are seldom read but always evaluated. It is more common for the bulletin to be read simply because it focuses on headlines, dates, and bullet points. This has cross-gender appeal. I say this because it is a long-standing truism in marketing that men read headlines and women read the details. Of course, this is not universally exact, but it is quite common. A good brochure or printed piece will connect with both, allowing headliners to get the gist of it all and allowing those passionate about the details to get their fill.

All printed materials that are available to communicate essential details about your church make up your church's personality in printed form. If your printed materials are inconsistent in style and quality, that pretty much is what people will subconsciously, or consciously, take away about the church. And to the extent that your materials are outdated or have photos with hairstyles from another decade, you are saying that about yourself as well. On the flip side, you might attempt to use these pieces to resonate as the "cool" church. It works if you have genuine appeal as the cool church. If you are not that, it can leave an awkward disconnect. You can easily come across looking like a poser—someone who is trying to compensate for not being happy with who they really are—trying to be cool when you are not. All of that said, you can and should have contemporary, relevant materials that create a bridge between your style and values as a church and those same lifestyle issues in your target community. In doing so design consistency, or branding, as we will get to later in the book, is your catalyst to a stronger sense of self that, if well targeted, will enhance a sense of belonging with your target audience right from the start.

> All printed materials that are available to communicate essential details about your church make up your church's personality in printed form.

### Attire of Leadership/Members

Similar to the cars in the parking lot, attire tells a story. The visible culture of the church is a vivid confirmation of what is valued by the congregation. Attire can be understated or played up. It is something your visitors are certain to notice, because they can, and will, quickly compare how they look against the church members. It will leave a taste in their mouths, good or bad.

### Doctrine

Even people who do not know much about church have often heard a lot about doctrine. It is often more important to a visitor in more church-saturated areas and less important in areas where fewer people have made a commitment to Christ. Think about the famous "Got Milk?" ad campaign. If someone is not a milk drinker, all the advertiser (the Milk Board) cares about is that they try milk. If someone is already a milk drinker, the advertisers want them to try "our" brand. Playing up doctrinal differences can make people give up before they "taste and see that the LORD is good" (Ps. 34:8).

The only people who will respond well to a church that wears its doctrine on its sleeve are those who have already come to the same conclusion. Everyone else just won't get the point.

### Pastor/Minister

Often, much of what causes people to return is how they connect with the minister and the message. If they feel that the minister spoke directly to their position or perspective, they will gravitate toward him or her even if they do not agree with every point. The more points of connection they see with the minister from attire to lifestyle habits to number of children, the more they will feel connected. However, if they do not see that the minister's life and walk are enhanced because of a spiritual infrastructure, the number of connections they feel may not matter.

### Supporting Ministries (Children's, Youth, Nursery, etc.)

What visitors want to see from these aspects of the church is twofold—security and genuine care. Fun is the cherry on top. What they are looking for when they drop their children off is a strong sense their child will be safe and secure and warmly and sincerely accepted into the class as an individual. They want to hear you say the child's name and see you help the child become part of the group. After all, this child is not just another kid to your visitor. This is *their* child. They want people to make their child feel special. It speaks volumes if you do and particularly if you don't.

Just a few weeks ago, I asked some family friends how their church hunting was going, as I knew they were looking to get settled in a church. The wife responded that they had loved the ministry of a particular church but were very disturbed by how their small children were treated when they were dropped off for class. For several weeks in a row, the children's leader looked the other direction when they arrived at the door. My friends were forced to call for her attention and advise that they were there to drop off their children. She checked the children in without a smile and "mushed" them into the herd. The same routine occurred at pickup time, but then she was not the only one without a smile; the children were equally discontent. The result? While the pastor preached his heart out, these visitors who were sure to become workers in the church simply could not let their children grow up in a church with this environment. They moved on. The church will likely never know why.

### What People from Other Churches Say

People talk. Church people really talk. I often think the two fastest forms of media in the world for getting the word out on something are CNN and church people. Therefore, know your church is being and has been talked about. If there have been public problems in the past, deal with them forthrightly and move on as openly as possible. People would rather you own up to your humanity than pretend it never happened. Here's the deal with people from other churches. Your actions will either prove them wrong or right. Know what is being said and reinforce it if it is good and exemplify the opposite if it is bad.

If a church is trying to navigate away from long-standing perceptions about its attitude or culture, overcoming people's thoughts can be a real challenge. About a decade ago Las Vegas, known for all forms of debauchery and gambling, attempted to repaint itself with a new image. We began seeing commercials and programs emphasizing the "family friendly" town and the huge variety of family attractions. It worked on some levels.

However, after years of trying to beat this new drum, the town reverted to its bread and butter. It dropped the family pursuit and regressed to marketing based on its historical perception. The most recent campaign—"What happens in Vegas stays in Vegas." Ultimately, it was a lot easier to sell who they really are to people hungry for that lifestyle. To become the true family capital of entertainment would have required a deep-rooted change that would be hard to fathom.

*Perceptions that have been consistent for the long term require a long-term commitment to both actual change and the communication of that change.*

Perceptions that have been consistent for the long term require a long-term commitment to both actual change and the communication of that change. If this is an endeavor you must go through, note that starting with real change is a must—if people hear you talk about change and don't see it, your credibility is shot.

### Current Members

In many cultures, where you go to church says a lot about you. Some churches thrive because they count a number of influential people among their congregation. The reasoning goes if this or that prominent person goes there, it must be a good church. What people in your church wear, what they drive, who they are, where they live, and how they act all can have an impact on outsiders. The impact can be positive or negative; it can draw some and repel some. Know that sometimes these issues are more important to some people than anything else. Sometimes it is because they hunger for popularity, and sometimes it is because they struggle to belong. Either way, no one goes to church and does not see the people that sit around them (even if they pretend they don't).

In all these elements, the central point is that people are subconscious students of their surroundings. Right or wrong, they notice, process, and evaluate a world of stimuli around them—from the parking spaces to the pulpit. And don't always assume people want to connect with affluence. Often it is just the opposite. People might be looking for a place where "packaging" doesn't matter. One way or another you are showing them what matters to you—and how much—by what you do or don't develop around you.

## Church Marketing Gone Wrong

In the first chapter, we discussed the high-tech firm that inadvertently showed its prospects "No one was willing to trust us with their microchips." Well, bad marketing like this is not uncommon, not in the secular world and not in the church world either. As I said earlier, "You only get one chance to make a first impression." That's all too true in both arenas.

For fun, let's look at some well-known, highly debated blunders of the marketing geniuses.

When Coca-Cola began selling in China in 1928, it first considered using the name Ko-ka-ko-la. Unfortunately, they discovered a little too late that the Chinese characters that made up the name actually translated to "bite the wax tadpole" or "horse stuffed with wax," depending on the dialect.

When Coors first attempted to use its slogan "Turn it loose" in Spanish markets, potential customers could have read it as "Suffer from diarrhea."

Clairol introduced the "Mist Stick," a curling iron, in Germany, only to find out that "mist" was slang for manure.

These folkloric examples illustrate an issue of trying to reach people with only a shallow understanding of their language, lifestyle, and culture. Church examples are not dramatically different. They also indicate a lack of proper translation in the minds of the unchurched.

The following are just a few that we have come across either in passing or in consulting reviews. And please, do not think I am trying to be "sassy." These are not really "funny" (although some should make us laugh). We love these churches and want them to reach their communities for Christ. I just want us to look at how we sometimes say things that we do not know we are saying. See if any of these examples pertain to churches you have visited.

A church wondered why it could not retain men in their congregation. The sanctuary was decorated with pink walls, pink carpet, and gold bows.

> Small problem: it is likely difficult for many men to commit to and bring friends to a church that is decorated like their daughter's bedroom.

A pastor of a two thousand-plus member church started a Sunday sermon by saying, "Do you remember what we talked about last week? Great, let's pick up there."

> Small problem: what if I am a first-time visitor? Now I feel like even more of an outsider. As well, I will have to try to follow the sermon without any context.

The pre-sermon announcer at an evangelistic event said, "As the minister comes to the podium, if anyone here does not have a Bible, please stand up."

> Small problem: as this was a publicized outreach event specifically intended to reach outsiders, the announcer inadvertently

made many of the people who already felt intimidated and out of place even further embarrassed by asking them to stand up and publicly admit that they did not know to bring a Bible (if they even owned one). Not to mention how those who brought these unknowing friends must have felt.

A highway church sign bore the message, "Sinners welcome here!"

Small problem: most people do not think of themselves as sinners. This invitation is likely to come across to the unchurched as meaning, "If you are really messed up, come here." That might not be a bad idea if your target market is really "messed up" people, but it is likely to drive away all those who do not realize that our need for God makes us all sinners. Responding to this sign is the equivalent to answering an altar call without hearing a message.

A church board intended to reach more "lost" people by using a logo showing "hands lifted up in the midst of fire," based on a theme of God's Spirit surrounding us in times of worship.

Small problem: to most unchurched (as well as most churched) people, "hands lifted up in fire" is more likely to indicate people burning in hell—not the most inviting image for the unbeliever.

An usher reprimanded a woman for her children's unruly behavior during a service. When she replied, "I'm so sorry; this is my first time here and I am a single mom," he said, "Why didn't you take them to the 'Cry Room'?" She replied she didn't know there was one.

Small problem: this woman, embarrassed by the attention her children have drawn and by the usher's reprimand, would undoubtedly have taken advantage of the "Cry Room" if she had known there was one. Inside the sanctuary, during the service is not the time and place to learn about child care options. In this case, a church with over eight thousand members did not have a single sign indicating there was a children's department. This leaves the newcomer with the definite impression that "People who do not already know how to find their way around our church don't matter to us."

A small church sets out three hundred chairs although their attendance has never broken forty.

Small problem: if while driving down a main street in your town you see eight restaurants completely packed and one with only two cars in front, what would you think about the almost empty one? Most likely, you would say, "There must be something wrong with that restaurant!" It is human nature and normal perception at work. A small group of people among hundreds of empty chairs often sends the message, "Something must be wrong with this place."

A small church uses a direct mail piece similar to one that a larger church in town sends out.

Small problem: if people are used to getting direct mail from another, larger church, they may well attribute your mailer to that church and not read it. You've just spent your money advertising for another church. That is not to say direct mail is a bad idea, even for small churches; just be distinguished and be consistent in being distinguished. Make your own mark!

A pastor provides an altar call at the end of the service, inviting "anyone who would desire to receive the atonement of the sacrificial covenant of the Lamb."

Small problem: without explanation, very few nonbelievers could translate that sentence into meaning, "Receive what Christ did for us." There might have been willing hearts whose minds could not grasp what was being asked.

Greeters talk among themselves and miss the opportunity to greet a first-time guest.

> Small problem: if I, as a visitor, see someone performing as a "greeter" and they do not greet me, I am likely to feel slighted and not welcome.

This list could be expanded to include even the more obvious perception shapers such as a teacher overheard being harsh to a child or the bad publicity that often follows a church leader's blatant sin. I am sure you can think of others.

In each of these real-life examples, everyone started out with the best of intentions. No one meant to make people feel out of place or to confuse visitors. These examples remind us to take stock of how we, at every point of contact, can make people feel, and how we shape their perception. There are so many things that shape perception. We have to be aware of them and shape our communication to achieve two goals: (1) to reflect the nature of Christ and (2) to be relevant to the community we are called to.

## Stumbling Blocks and Building Blocks

Consulting with ministries across the globe, we have witnessed countless little marketing speed bumps and stumbling blocks that keep people from ever clearly hearing the message of Christ in our churches. As the church, we do not mean to create them; often we have become just "churched" enough to overlook them—forgetting the perception of the person on the outside.

And please, do not mistake my observations and my passion for connecting with the lost for a desire to water down the gospel. Scripture reveals that Christ is either your cornerstone or your stumbling block. You either find his truths to be the foundation of your life or you stumble over them (1 Peter 2:7–8). Clearly, to some, Christ Himself will be a stumbling block. Therefore, you need to know in advance that not everyone will walk out of your church singing its praises. It is completely scriptural that you will not please everyone—but we must be sure that we are not creating stumbling blocks because of our inability to relate to and adapt ourselves (as Paul taught us) to the needs and understanding of the lost.

Remember Paul's words, "and to the Jews I became as a Jew, that I might win Jews; to those who are under the law, as under the law, that I might win those who are under the law" (1 Cor. 9:20). To reach people *we* have to adapt *our* lives and *our* approach to *them*. We must understand how they think, communicate, and perceive things. It is impossible to relate to someone without adapting our ability to communicate to his or her understanding.

And remember, the first church visit is quite possibly one of the most vulnerable moments in the entire lives of unchurched people. They feel so out of place, as if there is a big sign over their heads that says, "Look at me—I do not fit in!" And if you think just walking into a new church can be difficult, consider the visit that results from an invitation. Talk about vulnerable! I get nervous when I recommend a restaurant to a friend. I worry, "If they do not like it, they will think I have bad taste." How much more severe is it when I invite them to church? If they do not like it, they might think I am a buffoon, a cult-member, or a person with weak intellect. It is this very worry behind the saying, "People are not ashamed of Christ, they are ashamed of their church." Ouch!

> People are not ashamed of Christ, they are ashamed of their church.

What we often miss in these failures to connect is much more than just the opportunity with the visitor who walks through the church door. We also miss the opportunity for members to *bring* people through the doors, because their experience warns them that a disconnect is the probable result. Tens of thousands of churches have lost momentum in church growth because of this issue alone. If you are there, don't worry—we'll soon tackle how to get back on track, as God desires to remove all the roadblocks and replace them with on-ramps toward the knowledge of Christ.

## Moving Forward

Where do we go from here? So many things affect people's perception of your church; some are within your control and some are not. When we begin to consider what we are "showing them" in the little things, maybe we can understand why people do not see our churches the same way we do. We often see our intentions; they only see our follow-through. Your church might not be directly represented in any of the marketing mistakes we talked about, but most likely you are starting to see where the problems and the successes can occur. Let's take a second to sharpen our swords before we move on to making plans for real marketing success.

> When we begin to consider what we are "showing them" in the little things, maybe we can understand why people do not see our churches the same way we do. We often see our intentions; they only see our follow-through.

1. Realize that marketing is a huge team sport. It is a church-wide effort that requires church-wide buy-in. The more everyone is involved in communicating the same message or the same spirit, the more likely it is that your desired message will be conveyed. Are you willing to commit the time and money needed to represent your church well to others? What will your effort look like? Who will be a part of it? How will you teach and train your staff? Your volunteers? How will you emulate it in what you do?
2. Realize that it is often the little things we communicate without even knowing that can make the big difference. If you haven't done it, go back through the section titled

"Reading between the Lines" and jot down what you think you might be showing people without realizing it—the good and the bad. Take some time and look from the outside in on how you come across. Write down specifics, pool your thoughts with your leadership team, and then summarize your evaluation. Let this evaluation represent your current picture of how people see you—enlist some outsiders to help if needed.

3. Remember that Paul challenges us to adapt our message to the perspective of our audience. That means it is not all about us. It is not about making our church look great in the eyes of other churches—although this is a remarkably common motive. What is popular in church culture often has no connection with the world. This is about them. This is about those outside our church walls who are lost without Christ. Our efforts should not be self-centered but focused on others. Ultimately, great marketing is the end result of caring enough to do things right to further the cause of Christ in the lives of those around us. With that in mind, why would someone choose to visit your church? What draws people to you? Ask your members. Why did they come? Why did they stay? What is it about you that would make your community think you have the answer and you would welcome them in? What sets your church apart?

How can you better communicate these answers in all you do?

What things in your service might be a stumbling block for a non-Christian?

What can you do to help ensure an unbeliever is not distracted from the opportunity to hear the message of Christ?

Be open. If your church has derailed its visitors in the past, now is a good time to change. Write down your thoughts. Consider how connected you are as a church with those you desire to reach. We'll get deeper into these topics as we go along.

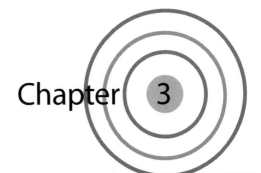

Chapter 3

# Perceiving Their Perception

In chapter one we defined marketing as the management of perception. We also discussed that management requires us to know where we are, to know where we are going, and to make adjustments along the way. The first thing we have to do is determine where we are as it relates to how we are perceived—no small task. This is an act of research, introspection, and insight. It is important that we deal with the reality of how people see us—as the body of Christ, as individual churches, and as individual believers in Christ.

In challenging you to explore these issues, I must share with you my feeling that being critical of your church or leadership is wrong. In no way do I condone or advocate people sharing their opinions in subversive ways. If, by analysis, you begin to see people as roadblocks, I challenge you that you are missing it. I further challenge you that it is the Holy Spirit's job to reveal certain things to His people and that unsolicited advice is seldom welcomed and treads on spiritual thin ice. A good rule of thumb is: if you are not directly responsible for the area of concern, communicate your thoughts only if called upon by those who are responsible. Sowing discord is counterproductive and abominable in the sight of God (Prov. 6:19). A simple way to make an impact without crossing the line might be to pass a copy of this book on to your leadership. If they have already read it or are in the process, relax and let God do the work. He's in charge. He'll get the glory. If you are still tempted in this area, I recommend the book *A Tale of Three Kings* by Gene Edwards as a directive on how to manage your opinion in light of God's orchestrated leadership.

That being said, if you are reading along at this point, I trust you are willing to commit your heart to the right track and to look at things objectively—handling gained insight with spiritual precision and being supportive of those around you.

## Man Looks on the Outside

"For the Lord does not see as man sees; for man looks at the outward appearance, but the Lord looks at the heart" (1 Sam. 16:7). We used this verse earlier to explain human nature. We are carnal and fleshly minded. Consequently, people often do not see us as we see ourselves. As I struggled for years to help churches understand the variances between their heart's intents and how their delivery was perceived, time and time again, God walked me through my own tests of this principle.

When we were a young marketing firm starting out in insane faith, obedience, and little else, my passion for "doing things right" and for getting our message out often turned me into an ogrelike persona. My catchphrase was always "know my heart." But honestly, it was hard to "know my well-intentioned heart" when my tone and delivery were oftentimes tyrannical at best—causing employees to walk away in tears. I had a personal marketing problem. My actions created a stronger perception than my heart did. That will pretty much always be the case, because man looks on the outside. It is the nature of God alone to see through our delivery and our packaging to the heart. If you have been in any form of leadership you have learned repeatedly that those you expect to "know your heart" fail time and time again to do so.

If the seasoned Christians around us have a hard time seeing through our actions to our heart, how much more intentional must our actions be for those outside our church walls. They do not know our hearts; even worse, they often distrust us and are skeptical of us from the beginning. A million personal experiences have shaped their perception of us as Christians and of our churches. We will have to work hard to change those perceptions.

Let's think back on some of the things that create perception. In the last chapter we mentioned denomination, website, curb appeal, décor, promotional materials, greeters, past events, the sermon, and more. You might think that managing each of these aspects to where they create a favorable impression is close to impossible. It's not. It does take a huge concerted effort, but it's not impossible. History tells us there was a place of worship that created a tremendous impression on a most discriminating and affluent first-time visitor.

The place of worship was the temple of Solomon and the visitor—the queen of Sheba. First Kings 10 tells us that she traveled afar because she had heard of Solomon's wisdom. She arrived with an entourage to test his knowledge with a life full of questions. In the simplest of terms, she needed to see how God's Word applied to her life. Sounds like a first-time visitor, right?

> And when the queen of Sheba had seen all the wisdom of Solomon, the house that he had built, the food on his table, the seating of his servants, the service of his waiters and their apparel, his cupbearers, and his entryway by which he went up to the house of the LORD, there was no more spirit in her. Then she said to the king: "It was a true report which I heard in my own land about your words and your wisdom."
>
> 1 Kings 10:4–6

Wow! So how Solomon's ushers dressed mattered? How the building was built mattered? How the greeters greeted mattered? How the entryway was organized mattered? You better believe it! To this queen, they were all evidence that validated the reality of God at work in Solomon's temple. Notice it says she "had seen all the wisdom of Solomon." How do you "see"

How the entryway
was organized mattered?
To this queen,
they were all evidence
that validated the reality
of God at work in
Solomon's temple.

wisdom? Every aspect of the temple and its people were managed and trained to create this impression. She was convinced before she even heard Solomon speak. She goes on . . .

> "However I did not believe the words until I came and saw with my own eyes; and indeed the half was not told me. Your wisdom and prosperity exceed the fame of which I heard. Happy are your men and happy are these your servants, who stand continually before you and hear your wisdom! Blessed be the LORD your God, who delighted in you, setting you on the throne of Israel! Because the LORD has loved Israel forever, therefore He made you king, to do justice and righteousness." Then she gave the king one hundred and twenty talents of gold, spices in great quantity, and precious stones. There never again came such abundance of spices as the queen of Sheba gave to King Solomon.
>
> 1 Kings 10:7–10

Pretty impressive. She did not "believe the words until" she "came and saw." This powerful first-time visitor looked (on the outside) at every detail and came to these conclusions: (1) I am empty inside, (2) God is real, (3) Solomon (the pastor) is wise, (4) the temple is even better than what people were telling me, and (5) people who go to that temple should be proud of their leader and happy to be there. She followed up her spiritual conversion by giving the largest offering in church history.

> She did not "believe the words until" she "came and saw."

Right about now you are either saying, "Bring it on, Lord!" or "Well, that is because God made Solomon so wise and they had such a huge budget and . . ."

As for Solomon's wisdom, it was great, but it pales in comparison to the wisdom we have found in Christ. Your church might not have Solomon's budget, but you can still shape what you do have into an instrument that glorifies God. After all, wisdom, service, excellence, and joy should be able to shine through even the most dilapidated church building. I have been invited to many a church where someone commented, "Please excuse the old building—just wait till you hear the incredible worship." I have never heard someone say, "Please excuse the out-of-tune music—just wait until you see how beautiful the building is." The building matters if you can do something about it. If you can't, it doesn't. Some of the greatest churches in the world were established in some of the least attractive places. Sharpen what you can sharpen—leave the results up to God.

What the queen of Sheba saw was inspiring; it was the fruit of God's presence. One of the main reasons some churches multiply in size while others struggle to see an ounce of growth is the spirit of excitement (synergy) generated when multiple aspects of the church service combine to create the perception of a church alive with something far beyond this universe. It is all spawned by people's perception.

I am not advocating all types of radical growth. I applaud growth if it comes by changing lives—not if it is just growth by Christians switching churches. Perception management is a true and valid principle. The world uses it all the time. It affects what kind of car you buy, what sports team you root for, what neighborhood you live in, or even if you choose not to live in a certain neighborhood. Perception management is powerful stuff; use it to honor God and boost people's perception of Him.

Your walk with God should speak for itself—as in Acts 4:13: "Now when they saw the boldness of Peter and John, and perceived that they were uneducated and untrained men, they marveled. And they realized that they had been with Jesus." There's that word *perceived* again. Funny. Peter and John overcame the people's perception of their ignorance by being full of God. That's some perception management.

> Remember, the world looks on the outside. So what is your church showing them?

Remember, the world looks on the outside. So what is your church showing them?

## Processing Perspective

I heard a great illustration that helps demonstrate how the unchurched process church. The reason I bring it up is that God, in His goodness, enables us to have such new lives in Him that we often lose track of what it felt like to be on the outside looking in. I am not sure to whom to credit this story, but I admit to have stretched it quite a bit since it was told to me. I've tested the principle it reflects with pastors in remotest Africa and believe it's quite universal.

Here goes.

Let's suppose you and I are good buddies, and you are the world's biggest baseball fan. I, on the other hand, find baseball to be mind-numbingly boring. After all, how much fun can you have watching a sport that has only three variables: the batter misses it, kind of hits it, or hits it right? Not enough options for me. I've never been to a game before, but I am sure that I will not like it. You beg me all the time to come with you. I really wish you would stop asking, but one day, I am weak and decide to give in to your request.

If I am going to this game with you, you had better be sure that you're buying my $2 nosebleed tickets and my hot dog. Together we sit in the upper deck on a hot afternoon—you in bliss and me in a sort of bewildered agony. I'm eating a hot dog and slurping a soft drink when all of a sudden the home team hits a home run. We jump to our feet together and high-five each other. I'm caught off guard. The hit inspired me. Maybe I like baseball after all. Am I actually enjoying a baseball game? This is not what I expected.

You ask me to go again and I commit. This time, I am buying my own cheap upper deck tickets and my own hot dog. I am willing to spend a little bit, but not enough to sit down in the lower deck with those $80/seat baseball freaks. They are a little too committed for me at this point. I think I like baseball, but my commitment level is low.

After returning for a number of games in my cheap upper deck seats and watching the home team knock home run balls out of the park, my passion for baseball builds. Those $80 seats now do not seem so expensive. After all, I might be able to catch a foul ball down there. I now have a jersey, a hat, and a leather glove. I am a huge fan. I solidify my passion by getting season tickets to ensure I never miss an inning. People at work know I am a fan. I talk a lot of baseball now. One day I even decide to join a softball league. It is a great way to get active. I look forward to playing any time I can. I even want to teach my kids how to play.

Each step along the way I committed more. I was skeptical at first, but now I am committed to give all. I did not get here overnight. I got here in steps.

These are the same steps many people go through when it comes to accepting Christ and becoming part of a church. Isn't that your story? I used to think I would never set foot in a church. A friend pleaded and shared his or her passion for Christ with me. I finally agreed to come to church and when I sat there, just like the queen of Sheba, I felt empty and full at the same time. I saw that there was something more. The pastor spoke words that hit a home run in my heart. They inspired me. I returned. I committed my life to Christ. I bought the high-priced seat—the seat of commitment and accountability. I bought the Christian T-shirt and the leather Bible. God was working in my life. People at work began to see a change. They learned that I had become a Christian. I solidified my commitment with membership. I even started inviting people to church. One day God called me onto the playing field. He challenged me not just to sit in a seat but also to participate. I now look forward to making myself available to serve any time I can. I can't wait to see my friends, family, and children come to Christ.

Disconnected outside the ballpark. Evaluating in the upper decks. Committed in the lower deck. Active on the playing field. Sometimes, as He did with the apostle Paul, God miraculously knocks you off your horse and you bounce from outside the

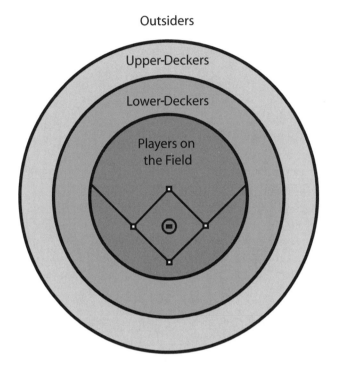

Outsiders

Upper-Deckers

Lower-Deckers

Players on
the Field

ballpark onto the playing field quite quickly, but most of the time people follow a similar progression over time. During this progression, God works with us to change our perception.

Now that we as the church know He is doing this, what can we do to help those outside the ballpark make it into the upper decks? What can we say to work with God to get those upper-deckers to commit to the lower deck? And what can we do to challenge those in the lower deck to step onto the playing field and contribute to the team?

I trust that you have seen this parallel I've drawn and that you understand I am not attempting to trivialize the kingdom of God with this baseball illustration. I simply desire that we understand people's perceptions come from various perspectives. We will be most successful if we learn to aid people right where they are—unbelievers or scholars, let us always challenge them to

# Some Definitions

**Outsiders:** Outsiders are those in your community who are not currently in church. This spans the spectrum between those who have never been introduced to church, to those who have been and never felt a connection, to those who have been disenfranchised. Our goal in promotional efforts is to connect with them and give them a glimpse of what they might value inside the church. Fundamental to that is our effort to make the service attractive to them when they come as upper-deckers to ensure that members feel comfortable inviting them.

**Upper-Deckers:** Upper-deckers include not only first-time visitors, but any who are in evaluation mode regarding the church. They are hesitant to commit and are trying to get a feel to determine if church in general is for them, and more specifically if your church is a fit for them. They need to feel compatible socially with the congregation and also that the ministry relates to where they are in life while holding the keys to something more. It is important that we let them process during the evaluation period but also provide them with a call to go deeper, because if they never commit to the lower deck, they will ultimately disconnect. The rule in our approach with the upper deck should be patience, but not passivity.

**Lower-Deckers:** Lower-deckers are those who have made a commitment to Christ and to your church. They have accepted membership as a responsibility or are acting like members through attendance and likely giving. Their greatest needs are for discipleship, teaching, and fellowship to solidify their foundation. Similar to the upper-deckers, it is expected that people will spend a significant amount of time settling into a more committed life. They also need patience, but not passivity. If they spend too long in the lower deck without getting onto the playing field (volunteering, training for leadership, etc.) they lose out on the deepest part of Christian growth and the church struggles to fill the need for ministry workers.

**Players on the Field:** These players represent those that have accepted the call to get involved; to make a difference and to take on new skills and invest their lives into others. A healthy church will provide various levels of volunteer opportunities to provide them with room to grow and the ability to season and hone their gifts.

rise to the next level. Let us consider each of these groups—their perspectives, their feelings, and their emotions—when we begin our marketing plans and also when we are considering our sermons. For example, are our sermons appropriate for those just stepping in from outside the ballpark? The upper-decker? God loves the upper-decker. How about the lower-decker? Perhaps we are only preparing messages for the players on the field. It is easy to do so. We hear their cheers the loudest.

## Sitting in Their Seat

Now let's cap off this illustration. After years of playing, a great talent begins to develop. From Little League through college and now to the big leagues—let's picture this rising star. He's Nolan Ryan. He's Roger Clemens. He's Randy Johnson. It's game seven of the World Series. The President of the United States threw out the first pitch to start the game. A Grammy award winner sang the most incredible national anthem you have ever heard. The game has been a seesaw battle. It's the bottom of the ninth inning. Everything is on the line. Randy Johnson is on the mound. This is the moment of a lifetime. He has thrown every pitch in his arsenal and his fans are rooting him on. Years have built up to this. He has eaten, drunk, and slept baseball. All his friends love baseball and love and admire him for how he plays the game. It is a full count. There are two outs. A strike and we win. Anything else might mean disaster. People from around the world are tuned in to watch this pitch.

At this moment, do you honestly think that Randy Johnson remembers what it feels like not to give a flip about baseball? Do you think he can relate to someone who has never been to a game, or heard the crack of a bat, or smelled the leather of the ball? Similarly, do you think every pastor who has lived his life on the spiritual infield, who has eaten, drunk, and slept church, whose friends love God and love and admire him for how he preaches, whose words yield applause by the syllable, remembers at all what it was like to be a stranger to church and to not know God? Do you think he remembers what it was like to hear the words of life for the very first time?

I pray we never forget what is going on in the lives of those in the seats farthest away. These visitors are often the most overlooked and least connected with on any given Sunday. After all, those closest to the playing field can tend to steer us by applause, but a good pitcher learns how to make the game great for people at all levels.

Jesus understood this. He was an expert on reaching people in their seats and always challenging them to stretch. Remember His ministry to the multitudes in John 5–6? Jesus challenged them with parables and word stories. He even fed them. A miracle played the part of a home run for all to see. He was inspiring the upper deck. He went across the lake; not all followed Him, but many did. They took the next step. They committed more and made it to the lower deck. He taught them there. He increased the depth and intensity of His ministry. Many lingered. It was time for Him to see who was in the lower deck and who would step onto the playing field. His next sermon topic was of eating human flesh and drinking blood. These were inner-court words. Deep words. Spiritually discerned words. Only His lifers could handle His sayings.

> Jesus adjusted His topics and His preaching style to His audience. He put Himself in their shoes and spoke on their level. He sat in their seats.

Jesus had different ministry styles based on whom He was connecting with at the time. He ministered to people where they were, but He was always challenging them to advance to the next level in their faith. He adjusted His topics and His preaching style to His audience. He put Himself in their shoes and spoke on their level. He sat in their seats.

## Re-engineering the Church Promotion Process

The summer between high school graduation and my first year of college, I worked for a friend at church who cleaned offices. We cleaned at night, usually from 8:00 p.m. until about 2:00 or 3:00 a.m. Cleaning is one of the least fun things in the world for me. As a matter of fact, I am amazed that my mother did not pass out at the thought that I would do for others what I had neglected to do for myself for about eighteen years. The funny thing is, I was pretty good at it. I mean, we never heard much in the form of praise from our clients, but in my own mind, I was a master cleaner.

I had adapted my own way of cleaning. I know this is crude, but to make my point I am going to chat about toilets for a second. When I went into these offices to clean the toilet stalls I was sure I was the best. Why? Simple. I watched the other people who cleaned them, and they followed this approach: open the stall door, wipe down the doors, spray the toilet, and they were done.

My "superior" method was this: I opened the stall and sat on the toilet lid. From there I had the most important perspective that exists in the bathroom world—the perspective of the person on the seat. After all, the person sitting there usually has time to stare at the walls. I can clean all day long, but if the stall is not clean from the view of the person on that seat, we have problems. Honestly, very few other perspectives matter. I would finish by wiping down the seat and voila! The cleanest toilet stall around.

With that in mind, some of us in ministry need to change seats. We need to look at the church all over again from the perspective of the first-time visitor. Things might look good when you are standing at the door, behind the pulpit, or in the youth room, but the bottom line at the end of the day for the church is how we come across to the person in that seat.

I have heard of pastors who dressed up as homeless people, panhandling in front of their church. Many were disgusted by how their unknowing congregations and staff treated them. Oh, what they learned by changing seats.

Man looks on the outside. Maybe we need to do the same for ourselves just to understand what they see.

Occasionally we hear from a church that spent years trying to develop the perfect slogan, believing it would be a key to growth. I have heard some say, "We have spent hundreds of hours in meetings trying to figure out who we are, what our core Scripture is, and how we should define ourselves to our community." They often spend thousands of dollars coming up with slick brochures and elaborate campaigns to communicate who they see themselves as: "The Church of Belonging," "The Church of Hope," "The Church of Power," "The Church of the Uncompromised Word." Often those outside their walls hear it and say, "So what? What good does that do me?"

> Man looks on the outside. Maybe we need to do the same for ourselves just to understand what they see.

How much time did those churches spend getting to know people in their community who were lost? How much time did they spend getting to know their needs, their hopes, their joys, and their pains? Did they find out what the lost needed from the church? Did they eat with them as Jesus would have? Did they step out to see the church from the perspective of those people—to engage with them around what is important to *them*? The world is full of churches that have built great campaigns out of a sense for who they were while never recognizing that the community at large simply did not care who they thought they were. It wasn't relevant to their needs. The churches got all dressed up for their prom but forgot to court and invite a date.

Don't get me wrong. It is critical to know who you are as a church—but who you are is only effective if it gives you the ability to connect with people where they live. Become one to win one. Connect the dots between you and them.

How do you reengineer the church promotion process? As church leaders, you start with where the people are. You adapt to their level. You sit in their seats. You "become all things to all men, that [you] might by all means save some" (1 Cor. 9:22).

## Moving Forward

If we first understand that "man looks on the outside," we can actually enhance our ability to connect with people. We saw that exemplified with Solomon's church and his first-time visitor, the queen of Sheba.

We also talked about ministering to people on different spiritual levels. It is natural for people to evaluate as upper-deckers, commit as lower-deckers, or be active as players on the field. We shouldn't expect people to behave any differently. So how can we use that knowledge to enhance the experience for people at all levels?

In order to see what they see, we have to change positions. I challenge you to step outside your church for a moment and see it all over again for the first time. Be an unchurched person in your community. Just for a moment put on their life challenges and preconceived ideas.

Now how do you see the church? How do you feel? Write it down.

Is it inviting or intimidating? How would you feel if you were from a lower social class? A higher one? Would you know where to go once you parked? How should you dress? Where do you drop off your children? Are you greeted like a VIP or made to feel like an outsider? Take a moment to document the things you do to make visitors feel at home. Go even further. What could you do to make them feel as if you built the whole experience just for them? Could you make them feel like the queen of Sheba felt even before she heard the message?

Would you understand what is being said inside? Would ministry take place that inspired you as an upper-decker? Challenged you as a lower-decker or a player on the team? Would you hear the "crack of the bat" and see that church can be more than you expected? Is there life-changing wisdom inside for everyone?

Write down what visitors would think about your church. Talk about it as a team.

Now write down what you want them to think.

Brainstorm what you might have to do to make this connection on each level.

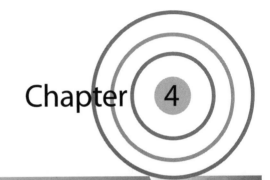

Chapter 4

The Biblical Foundation for Target Marketing • Dealing with Demographics • Basic Human Needs • Calculating Psychographics • Lingering with the Masses • Moving Forward

# Understanding Your Target Markets

A number of years back, a church called our marketing firm and told us they were opening a Christian high school; they wondered if we would help them design a "cool" T-shirt to help get young teens excited about their new school. It was a somewhat unusual request. I remember that I was immediately concerned about the concept of relying on a T-shirt to stir up excitement.

I spoke with the associate pastor who was leading the school launch. His church had already spent over $150,000 on marketing for this launch with a different agency, yet with only a couple of months until launch they had garnered only two interested students. They needed thirty-two to break even. I could feel the frustration in his voice. This five thousand-plus member church had stuck its neck out to fulfill a heartfelt vision of launching a high school. I asked the associate pastor, whom I considered to be very sharp, to send me a sampling of the materials they had been using for promotion.

When I received the materials, I knew the problem. I called him back and advised that we would not be interested in designing the shirts. He was immediately flustered. I told him that his problem could not be solved with a T-shirt and that he needed a marketing plan. The problem, he voiced, was that their previous plan had burned their budget and did not work. On a wing of faith and tenacity we offered to fly down there and perform a number of focus groups and develop a plan for them. If they deemed our insight and direction to be worth it, they would pay our expenses and our fee. If they did not, we would swallow the costs. How could they refuse?

Making a long story short, we spent a day and a half studying junior high students (the potential students for the new high school) and understanding their world. We developed a plan based on what we knew would illuminate the school to them and seal the deal.

We helped them to see that the specific group of Christian teens they were looking for, at large, had the clout (earned or unearned) with their parents to make the decision on where they went to high school. Our plan outlined a communication strategy, a specific "look," and a specific set of promotional methods. It called for spending less than $10,000 on strategic communication that would connect the hearts of these teens and their parents to the new school the church had envisioned.

We executed the plan. The school launched less than two months later with thirty-six students. The principal wrote us a letter thanking us for our help in saving their high school.

> There is no substitute for understanding your target market. Not understanding it is oh so costly.

Today it is a flourishing testament to Christian education. I recently visited and saw our executed design and communication strategy beautifully fulfilled in almost every aspect of the school. The energy was palpable. The students were proud of their school. I was introduced in a Spanish class as the owner of the firm that made their school so cool. The teens gave a standing ovation. I cried. There is no substitute for understanding your target market. Not understanding it is oh so costly.

## The Biblical Foundation for Target Marketing

If marketing is the management of perception, then what is target marketing? Webster tells us the "target" is "one to be influenced or changed by an action or event." Combining these two would tell us that target marketing is taking specific aim to manage the perception of a person or group. I know you're wondering how this plays out biblically. So here goes . . .

Let's look one more time at Paul's words, "and to the Jews I became as a Jew, that I might win Jews; to those who are under the law, as under the law, that I might win those who are under the law; to those who are without law, as without law (not being without law toward God, but under law toward Christ), that I might win those who are without law; to the weak I became as weak, that I might win the weak" (1 Cor. 9:20–22).

Why didn't Paul just say, "I will be all things to all people" without spelling it all out? It seems he was taking time to categorize people deliberately—grouping people with common tendencies together. After all, not all Jews are alike. Not all weak people have the same weakness. Paul was doing two things: (1) he was indicating that not all people were viewing the gospel from the same perspective, and (2) he was saying that certain types of people tended to think alike or have a similar perspective.

Paul was not prejudging them. He was not negatively stereotyping them. He was, however, categorizing them based on perspective and lifestyle. I cannot believe I just wrote that! But read it for yourself; it's true! He grouped people based on ethnic background (Jews), spiritual devotion (under the law), spiritual ignorance (those who are without the law), and psychological and/or economic needs (the weak). Finding out what lifestyle pattern people lived in helped Paul connect with them on their level.

When you think of Paul's ministry, is it any wonder that he became adept at reaching people of different backgrounds? If you look at his travels in the book of Acts, you'll see that his ongoing communication with people from the different areas he touched is crystal clear. Look at Paul's ministry in Athens . . .

Then Paul stood in the midst of the Areopagus and said, "Men of Athens, I perceive that in all things you are very religious; for as I was passing through and considering the objects of your worship, I even found an altar with this inscription: TO

THE UNKNOWN GOD. Therefore, the One whom you worship without knowing, Him I proclaim to you: God, who made
the world and everything in it, since He is Lord of heaven and
earth, does not dwell in temples made with hands."

Acts 17:22–24

There goes Paul perceiving again. What a brilliant job. Notice
that he did not blast them for their many idols and false gods.
In order to have an opening to communicate the One True God,
Paul actually complimented them on their many gods. Oh my!
Does that not blow your mind? His ministry bore fruit and he
moved on to Corinth . . .

> So, because he was of the same trade, he stayed with them and
> worked; for by occupation they were tentmakers. And he reasoned
> in the synagogue every Sabbath, and persuaded both Jews and
> Greeks.

Acts 18:3–4

Can you believe this? Paul, the great minister who wrote two-
thirds of the New Testament, is hanging out building tents just
to disciple people on their level. Then when he preached his
sermons, he related specifically to people of Jewish mind-set
and also packaged a portion of his ministry in context with the
Greek mind-set.

Paul traveled from town to town ministering in a variety of
different ways and adjusting his approach and reasoning based
on his audience. In Jerusalem, his perception of the crowd and
his quick response took him even further.

> Then as Paul was about to be led into the barracks, he said to the
> commander, "May I speak to you?" He replied, "Can you speak
> Greek? Are you not the Egyptian who some time ago stirred
> up a rebellion and led the four thousand assassins out into the
> wilderness?" But Paul said, "I am a Jew from Tarsus, in Cilicia,

a citizen of no mean city; and I implore you, permit me to speak to the people."

Acts 21:37–39

Further on . . .

But when Paul perceived that one part were Sadducees and the other Pharisees, he cried out in the council, "Men and brethren, I am a Pharisee, the son of a Pharisee; concerning the hope and resurrection of the dead I am being judged!"

Acts 23:6

After baffling the crowd by using his insight into the group's contrasting perspectives on the topic of resurrection, he won points using Greek and by managing the commander's perception of who he was. He went on from there to speak Hebrew to the crowd and won their complete attention. To top it off, in Acts 22:28, he told his accusers he was a Roman citizen, which stymied their prosecution and opened doors for him to move forward in his destiny.

The story of Paul reminds me of an excellent program I saw on PBS called *Merchants of Cool*. In this documentary, top American brands that marketed to teens shared their philosophies on how they learned to connect to America's "cool kids" in order to sell their products. A marketing executive at MTV shared, "We learned that the companies that win are the ones who learn to speak the kids' language the best." Now think about Paul. He constantly adjusted his message to match his target. He was adept at speaking their language, whether a dialect, a mentality, or a hot topic. He used it to shape perception, gain audience, draw attention, and produce respect in the minds of all who were around. Paul was a master target marketer.

> Paul was adept at speaking their language, whether a dialect, a mentality, or a hot topic. He was a master target marketer.

Further, Paul goes on to write letters to the people he had ministered to. Notice the variation in the letters throughout the balance of the New Testament. He did not copy the same letter over and over and send it to everyone he knew. He sent them letters based on where they were spiritually and in life. He did not scoff at those less spiritual; he challenged groups and individuals to move to the next level. His message to the Corinthians was decisively different than to the Romans or the Philippians. Why? Because Paul target marketed. Paul took specific aim to manage the perception of a person or group, based on where they were in life.

## Dealing with Demographics

We live in a time where our communities reflect what Paul saw on his trek across Asia. Gone are the days of four radio stations and three television channels. In almost every town, there is unparalleled diversity in mind-set and lifestyle—just as Paul experienced. Paul's audiences were dramatically fragmented—ethnically, mentally, economically, religiously, and culturally. Having insight into the lifestyles that exist in your community is paramount to connecting effectively with those outside your church. You'll find it will help you serve your congregation better as well.

> Having insight into the lifestyles that exist in your community is paramount to connecting effectively with those outside your church.

As we begin to categorize (like Paul did) we must remember it is an effort to learn about the people we are attempting to reach—to be able to see life and church from their eyes. We need to understand their frame of reference. For example, couples who have children see life differently from those who do not. People who grew up in wealthy households generally have a different perception of the world around them than do those who have been reared below the poverty line. Military families who move frequently look at things differently than nonmilitary families who raise children in the same house their parents raised them.

How can we better understand this variety of lifestyles? For one, demographics. According to Webster, demographics are "the characteristics of human populations and population segments, especially when used to identify consumer markets." Demographics are numbers. To the trained eye, they can tell volumes. They are not meant to replace personal interaction any more than studying a foreign language can make you fluent without immersing yourself in the culture. They can, however, give you insight into very interesting dynamics. They can tell if your community is broke, affluent, in debt up to their eyeballs, or financially passive. Demographics can give us insight into people's needs, lifestyles, and thought patterns.

Here are some examples of typical demographic data. You can generally find such data sectioned down to the zip code or neighborhood level in some form or fashion.

- Household income
- Population growth
- Age distribution
- Industry of labor
- Ethnic distribution
- Household size
- Number of autos
- Rent or own
- Year household built
- Cost of living
- Travel time to work
- Education level
- Tenure in home
- Migration patterns
- Mortgage as a factor of income
- Trends/changes in all of the above data over time

You could obtain countless more categories of data, but for most churches, this list would be a good start and is available at no cost from your local chamber of commerce and from the census details provided by the U.S. government (www.census. gov). You will also find valuable information by simply doing an Internet search for "demographics" and your county name. By compiling, reviewing, and mulling over the information you will begin to see definable patterns and trends. It is valuable and gives you relatively good information. Consider it like an election poll—close but not exact.

## Basic Human Needs

One of the quintessential aspects of understanding human nature is determining what people truly need. We know they ultimately all "need" more of God, but there are some basic physiological and psychological needs that all people have. A stellar resource on understanding human needs was developed in the 1930s by Abraham Maslow. It is not a "spiritual needs" chart. It is a chart of basic human needs and is very help-ful in categorizing what people are struggling with. His chart conjectures that people tend to have fundamental levels of need. Each level builds upon the level that preceded it. Keep in mind that this is not a doctrine, it is just a way of helping us categorize people's needs. It certainly is not holy, but it can be enlightening.

### *Maslow's Hierarchy of Needs*

#### Level One: Physiological Needs (Food/Clothing)
Need for relief from thirst, hunger
Need for sleep
Need for relief from pain
Need for biopsychosocial balance

### Level Two: Safety Needs (Shelter/Security)

Need for security
Need for protection
Need for freedom from danger
Need for order
Need for predictable future

### Level Three: Love and Belonging Needs (Affection)

Need for friends
Need for companions
Need for a family
Need for identification with a group
Need for intimacy

### Level Four: Self-Esteem Needs (Rank/Status)

Need for respect
Need for confidence based on good opinions of others
Need for admiration
Need for self-confidence
Need for self-worth
Need for self-acceptance

### Level Five: Self-Actualization Needs

Need to fulfill one's personal capacities
Need to develop one's potential
Need to do what one is best suited to do
Need to grow and expand meta-needs: discover
truth, create beauty, produce order, and promote justice

How does this affect target marketing? Let me bring this into context. When you are ministering to people who do not know where their next meal will come from, you are not connecting with them by telling them that God has great plans for their life. Teaching the "great plans for your life" message is trying to fulfill a level one need with a level five solution. Conversely, if you are speaking with an affluent group who have a strong sense of belonging (level three) and are truly self-confident (level four), you are not connecting with them when you tell them, "God can deliver you financially!" Your ministry to them on a level one or two need is not relevant.

In both cases the people are not in a position to handle this information. It will likely be seed that falls by the wayside, as the soil is not ready or is more compatible with different seed (Mark 4). A wise sower learns the characteristics of various soil types and knows to plant seeds that have a greater chance to take root.

---
A wise sower learns the characteristics of various soil types and knows to plant seeds that have a greater chance to take root.
---

Let's take a second to chew on this. What are the needs of your congregation? Are they level one, two, three, four, or five? It is highly unlikely that all five are represented in great numbers because people with level four needs usually do not spend time with people with level one needs and vice-versa, not even in the church. It's just not typical.

## Calculating Psychographics

Combining the use of the demographic data we discussed earlier with the evaluation of basic human needs is one way we can determine the lifestyle characteristics also called "psychographics." Webster tells us that psychographics are "the use of demographics to study and measure attitudes, values, lifestyles, and opinions, as for marketing purposes." In short, psychographics are how demographics translate into a person's lifestyle. Not all those who make $30,000/year have the same lifestyle. If you and I make the same amount and you live alone in an inherited, moderate house putting 30 percent in savings monthly, and meanwhile I own a 4,000-square-foot home that eats up 80 percent of my income and have a wife, four kids, and three cars—it is sufficient to say we do not have the same lifestyle. Our demographics may be similar in some areas but our psychographics (lifestyles) are worlds apart.

In learning about demographics and psychographics, you will begin to see that most people tend to fit lifestyle patterns. Chances are you are in one. Major marketing firms have seen the correlation between what music you like, what foods you eat, and what shoes you wear. And if you think that you break all the molds, well, I'm sorry to say there is also a mold for you. You are "the person who has decided to try not to fit any molds." Come on. Even nonconformity for the sake of being a nonconformist is just simply conforming yourself to nonconformity. I'm teasing a bit here, but it's true.

When I worked in the high-tech industry I remember chatting with a worldly salesperson. I was telling him that I loved coffee. He was a proud "Texas boy" misplaced in the Silicon Valley who said that he thought drinking coffee was a gimmick bought into by the weak—that it was a ploy to make people feel like they are smart and "belong." To him, people sitting around drinking coffee meant they were just giving in to a smug, yuppie mentality. Coffee did not even taste all that good. He was proud not to be one of those "followers." I knew him too well to let him get away with this "mightier than thou" attitude, so I simply asked him if he liked cigars. He said he loved them. There was nothing better than sitting around with a bunch of friends and tearing open a fresh cigar—what a feeling it gave him. He mentioned he could really bond with someone over a cigar. I just laughed. My coffee was his cigar. If I was a follower, so was he, and he just realized it.

Since belonging is one of the foundational human needs, even people who are living in higher needs categories have already established their sense of belonging and therefore tend to fit a lifestyle pattern. Common lifestyle patterns enable us to categorize people into lifestyle profiles.

While consulting at a large affluent church, I challenged the board by claiming that a common trait of people who attended their church was that they were discriminating, not ethnically but in areas of quality. Noting that the church was located in a woodsy community, I inferred that they were the type who did not wear "hiking boots," they wore "Timberlands." They did not have "sunglasses," they had "Oakleys." Offended by my observation, one of the members challenged me. "That's not true. We're not like that," he said. A colleague quickly reminded him that she had never heard him mention his ever-present bottle of water as anything other than "my Evian."

Paying attention to these lifestyle patterns helps us learn languages to communicate relevantly with the people in our communities. Often what it all boils down to is this: the church that speaks their language the best grows the fastest. Speaking their language means connecting personally and spiritually with them. It does not mean showing a video clip as an object lesson or borrowing a sermon series title from the name of the most recent box office hit.

> If your church is not relevant, a video clip, multimedia presentation, or catchy sermon title will not solve your problem.

If your church is not relevant, a video clip, multimedia presentation, or catchy sermon title will not solve your problem. I find it fascinating that many churches have decided that the use of video makes them more relevant. I am not against video clips. It's just that there are thousands of churches showing video clips that are not hitting home runs. Why? Because relying on the clips masks the fundamental problem of not meeting people where they live.

Listen, the reality is that we all like to belong. From sports teams to pickup trucks to country clubs and designer clothes, there is something most people cling to outside of themselves that gives them a sense of belonging, even if they rarely see it as such. It's inherent. It even happens inside the church—denomination to denomination; there are as many consistencies in lifestyle, hairstyle, and dress as there are with doctrine. Understanding lifestyle trends can give a great window into the mentality of people we are trying to reach—just like it did for Paul.

What has changed a bit since Paul's day is the added complexity of people groups—especially in the United States. The more complex a society becomes, with a greater variety of economic circumstances, ethnic backgrounds, and the added multiplicity of influences such as media or style, the more difficult it is to attribute group characteristics based on a single lifestyle factor. Paul was able to categorize based on ethnicity, but we most likely cannot. We cannot assume that the lifestyle of all people with a similar income is the same any more than we can assume that people with the same skin color are the same. In a more complex society, we have to break it down further. We have to categorize by grouped lifestyle characteristics. Remember when Paul mentioned the weak? He was generalizing a group of people. For us, we might generalize a group of people who are "living paycheck to paycheck" or are "keeping up with the Joneses."

Ultimately, it often helps to create personas that represent these characteristics. Think about how they live. What are the common characteristics of their lifestyles? Where do they shop? What do they drive? Where do they work? How many children do they have? What are their life challenges or their basic human needs? It might help you as a church to define made-up representatives of lifestyle groups. You might represent a group that spends over 50 percent of its income on mortgages as "House-broke Hal." Whether that helps you understand people better or not, it is important to be able to recognize, understand, and distinguish different psychographic groups and their lifestyle patterns.

## Lingering with the Masses

People often ask me, "How do you derive rich psychographic understanding from demographic data?" Well, categorical systems such as Maslow's Hierarchy of Needs are one means of understanding people's needs and lifestyles, but the best understanding comes from lingering with the masses. Observing people is one of my favorite activities. I love to go to the mall or to the airport and watch people. I look at the details (what color T-shirts the different teen groups are wearing) and at the big picture (how I would assess the people groups that I see at this mall compared to a mall across town). I watch which stores they go into. I evaluate the different stores and the different target groups. I pretend to be everyone's personal shopper and determine which store they would buy from and then from which section in that store. In the airport, I guess where people are going to and coming from. I read people by their shoes, their good-byes, their periodicals, and their luggage. I have matrices in my head of what makes people tick. I hope to be as good as Paul one day.

I am not a big believer in surveys. Surveys are good for learning quantifiable data such as "What percentage of our church membership has an Internet connection at home?" Surveys fall short in delivering qualitative data. Visitors will hardly ever share why they are not going to return to your church (unless something really makes them mad). Most of the time, they do not even know why. They could not circle it on a survey because they can't describe the disconnection between you and them, especially because the disconnection might reveal some of their hidden prejudices. That means we must become students of our target audiences as Paul was.

> Visitors will hardly ever share why they are not going to return to your church (unless something really makes them mad).

How did Paul know to tell the group of Pharisees and Sadducees that he was a Pharisee (Acts 23:6)? He knew it would trigger something in them because he knew their nature, their issues, and their debates. Why did he tell the Greeks that they were so religious (Acts 17:22)? Because he knew they were wise in their own minds and that his message would direct them toward the real God without pointing out how wrong they were. He was a quick read. He understood what made people tick. He was sensitive to it.

You have probably caught on by now that demographics and psychographics are just fancy words for "understanding people better." Just because Paul did not write an essay on the mentality of Greeks in relationship to their social discussion of idols does not mean he did not care enough to understand their frame of mind. He might not have written it down, but he stopped to think about it: "Now while Paul waited for them at Athens, his spirit was provoked within him when he saw that the city was given over to idols" (Acts 17:16).

Paul had made a lifestyle of being relational and understanding what made people tick. How did he minister to people in Corinth? He built tents with them (Acts 18:3). He lingered with them. Jesus did the same. He even hung out with sinners. Jesus responded to the "religious" who accused Him of not surrounding Himself with "holy" people. "'How is it that He eats and drinks with tax collectors and sinners?' [they asked]. He said to them, 'Those who are well have no need of a physician, but those who are sick. I did not come to call the righteous, but sinners, to repentance'" (Mark 2:16–17). Jesus was so centered. How can we reach those outside our walls if we don't spend time with them?

> How can we reach those outside our walls if we don't spend time with them?

The example above somewhat defines the two different approaches to the Christian's interaction with the world: (1) being around them to give relevant light as Jesus and Paul did, or (2) avoiding the world from a position of judgment.

I'll never forget a time when I was in undergraduate school and had driven home one weekend. I was headed out of church to meet some friends for lunch when I ran into someone I had never met. She was a short, withered woman, likely in her sixties, who looked as if she had been through a lot in life. Her skin was dark and rugged, and she smelled of cigarettes. She had only a few teeth and was out of place by many church standards. By her appearance I assumed she had seen many years of poverty. I could tell she hungered for attention, as she was quite talkative to me, a stranger. She was charming, and you could hear in her words that God had His hand on her life. I made a concerted effort to listen to her and ask her questions about herself. She and I stood outside her car for at least twenty minutes sharing stories of God's goodness.

Although I was late for my lunch appointment, I soaked in the moment. It was completely out of my element to be doing what I was doing. As we chatted she reached into her car to offer me a music cassette that had meant much to her. I could see that this might just be more than her car. This was likely where she lived as well. It was certainly a life I had never known.

We encouraged each other in the Lord a few moments longer and then she departed. Right before she left, she invited me to ride with her to a ministry event she had planned to attend over four hours away. At that moment, I remember thinking, "It would be like Jesus to go with her." My school and work prohibited it, but I truly considered it—knowing it would change how I saw my life and hers forever.

Lingering with the masses does two things: it changes how we see people and how people see us.

When I was in high school I had a life-changing experience with Christ. I went from being quite the party animal to becoming a Christian leader in my school. In spite of my growth, I had a recurring problem—the inability to get out of bed in the morning. I was a night owl. My brother had a remedy for this problem of mine. He would come into my room and yell, "Get up!" while turning on every light in my room.

Learning from this method, I used it to wake myself up one morning. I leaned out of bed to flip on a "blinding" light. My eyes were not adjusted. I could see red spots and immediately fell back into bed and closed my eyes. A few moments later I subjected myself to another blast from my bedside lamp. My eyes stayed open longer as I became more and more adjusted. After a while I was ready to get up—eyes wide open for the day ahead.

Something hit me as I struggled to adjust to the light. I realized this is what it is like when most people see God for the first time. Their eyes are accustomed to darkness. When they first see the light they often close themselves off to it. But after a while, as they experience more light, they begin to realize that they cannot live without it. It is essential to them. Their alternative is to close their eyes and go back to sleep.

The time and effort we spend in lingering with the masses will pay off in many ways. And yes, sometimes God gives them a blast of light, as He did Paul, that leaves them blind for a season while the light grows on them and in them (Acts 9:3–9).

## Moving Forward

What a heavy chapter! Let's look back for a second. We determined that nonjudgmental categorization is helpful and even biblical. We learned from Paul that categorizing based on such things as ethnicity, spiritual participation, doctrine, and needs is fair game. We discussed the value of demographic data, understanding basic human needs, and processing the two into psychographic (lifestyle) trends and therefore categories. We learned that we must become students of the people around us and learn how the details of their lives correlate into lifestyle trends. We learned that there is value in thinking about how to relate to people as well as spending time with various types of people in order to enhance our ability to minister to them.

It is important that we put some of these things together and begin to process them. We must open our eyes to the world around us like never before. Think about what people in your community are going through. Think about what is important to them. How does the message of Christ intersect with their needs in a "home run" way? Write it down.

Are your church's messages meeting people where they live? One thing to consider is that consistent ministry on topics related to the same type of personal struggles over time might be creating the type of crowd your church is reaching.

Does your crowd reflect your community? Does your community live lower or higher on the Hierarchy of Needs? If visitors from a different lifestyle or need level came in, would your building, your décor, your church culture, and the message connect with them where they live or would it only serve to reinforce the chasm that exists between them and church?

Describe the type of people your church is adept at reaching. Categorize them. Define their lifestyle, what goes on in their day. What are their cares and concerns? What makes them laugh?

Make a dedicated effort as a staff to linger with the masses. Make it an ongoing project. Learn what makes them tick. Share your insight with your team. Find out how to introduce light into their lives. Learn from it. Share your findings—what works and what doesn't.

What do they need from church? What do they think they need?

How can your church help them perceive this need without turning them off? Where are the open doors?

Create a number of profiles for the lifestyle categories that you consider your primary targets. Write down your ideas, observations, and conclusions.

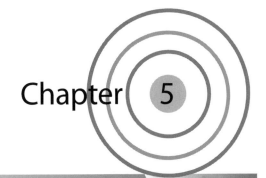

Chapter 5

# Fundamentals of Growth

Have you ever wondered why some churches have existed without an ounce of growth for ten years, where in the same community other churches have multiplied over ten times within twelve months?

Many church leaders have struggled with issues of growth for years. They have tried a multitude of promotional strategies, from door hangers to giving prizes for bringing visitors, and, unfortunately, these attempts have had little or no effect over time. Even worse, by promoting a church that was not seeing internal success, many have actually hurt their long-term opportunities for growth.

## Where Growth Comes From

One of the challenges to discussing church growth is that we do not all see eye to eye on what growth looks like. I have actually heard from churches large and small that believed they were the perfect size. They were not only content with not growing; they also were committed to it. Interesting, huh? Some churches feel that numbers do not matter. My general contention is that if numbers reflect souls, I have a hard time dismissing their importance. The whole argument reminds me of the "starfish story":

> My general contention is that if numbers reflect souls, I have a hard time dismissing their importance.

There was an older man in a small fishing village who woke early each morning to fulfill a special, self-given task. He made his way to the coastline to save the many starfish that were washed up on shore the night before. With the subsided tide they were guaranteed to lose connection with their life source, the ocean, and die within hours. Each morning, thousands were washed ashore. And while our friend could not save them all, he did his best to save as many as he could.

One day, a young tourist stopped the man and asked him, "Why do you work so hard to help these starfish? There are thousands. Surely you cannot save them all, and chances are many will be in the same predicament tomorrow. Why do you toil so, when you do not make a difference?"

The older gentleman was saddened by the words of the young man. He reached down, grabbed a starfish, and helped him safely back into the ocean. He looked at the man and said, "It made a difference to that one."

I know this is a sappy story, but I can relate to it. I am one of those starfish and so are you. I pray we have the heart of this older man and always think about reaching the people around us. It makes a difference. Conversely, I think growth only for the sake of numbers is deplorable, and I also think there are, in actuality, very few churches with that mentality; more often there are nongrowing churches that simply categorize growing ones as such. Much of the struggle comes because church growth is often seen as a by-product of decreased spirituality or increased emotionalism. It need not be either one. And even if you think that you do not want your church to increase in size, you can still use marketing principles to increase its "growth" in other areas.

Basically, there are two types of numerical growth: (1) lateral—growth by changing churches, changing doctrinal positions, or churchgoers relocating to a new area and (2) vertical—growth by evangelization and spiritual conversion. I guess there is, of course, a third type of growth that comes from having children, but I would hardly try to put a marketing plan together for that one.

## Origins of Lateral Growth

In the third chapter, I mentioned that growth by changing lives is much more applaudable than growth by Christians switching churches. Some of what creates today's larger churches is simply displacement from struggling ones. That is not always the case, but it is not uncommon. Larger churches generally have more to offer and can often make it easier on members to invite friends and expect positive outcomes. But that larger church had to start somewhere, and no church wants to be completely made up of lateral growth people because these church-transient believers can leave as easily, and quickly, as they arrived.

Another part of lateral growth comes from doctrinal change. Certain churches are excellent at winning people to Christ, while others are adept at winning Christians to their slant on doctrine. I am not even going to touch this topic. Just about every doctrinal stance thinks it's right and that conversion to its way of thinking is therefore good. So, I will just point it out because it exists as a form of growth.

For both of these areas of growth it is most important to focus on what your church is doing. If other churches in your area are growing, applaud them and support them. Chances are, every church in your community could double in size and you still would find less than 20 percent of the population in church on Sunday. Avoid the temptation to be stingy with souls. They don't belong to your church—they're God's. What's important is that, as a church, you are being sensitive to people and are preparing your church for growth. We will be discussing a number of ways to increase growth in the upcoming pages and chapters.

The last part of lateral growth comes through relocation or migrational changes. Population growth brings new people to your area who are looking for a church. This is quite a valid way for churches to grow. If your community is in a growth spurt, the key is knowing what makes Christians tick when it comes to choosing a new church. We'll cover this in the next chapter.

## Origins of Vertical Growth

When 0.000001 percent of a population is Christian, vertical growth is about your church's only option. That's what we saw with the disciples' first attempts at fulfilling the Great Commission. In Acts, thousands were added to the church on a daily basis. Acts 2:41, three thousand; Acts 4:4, five thousand; Acts 6:7, numbers multiplied; Acts 7:17, grew and multiplied; Acts 9:31, they multiplied; Acts 12:24, the Word grew and multiplied.

As Christians, hopefully we see our lives as instruments toward this same Great Commission. Therefore, I will assume we all want to see at least a fraction of the growth experienced by the early church—to be instruments for the Master's use. To be good stewards, let's look at how vertical church growth happens.

For the most part, there are two ways nonbelievers make it into an actual church: (1) by coming on their own and (2) by coming with a churchgoer. That pretty much covers it. Of course, people can also watch your church services on television or the Internet and that's all good, but that is a whole topic unto itself. Even the growing usage of small groups as a way to assimilate people into the congregation has the same contingencies that the church does—it's just a microcosm with the same issues and more personal interaction. With that said, I think we are safe with looking at these two ways.

> Think about the non-churchgoers. One Sunday morning they decide, "Today is the day we will go and see what church is like." Think this was an easy decision? No way. This was quite possibly one of the hardest decisions they've made in their lives.

### The Uninvited Visitor

Think about the non-churchgoers. One Sunday morning they decide, "Today is the day we will go and see what church is like." Think this was an easy decision? No way. This was quite possibly one of the hardest decisions they've made in their lives. They are about to undergo the most intimidating experience in the world. They are somewhere they have never been that is full of people they assume grew up there. They do not understand the church language and do not know where to go. They might have come because they felt, "Our kids need to be in church," yet they do not know where the children's department is. Everyone else is carrying a Bible, but they do not have one. So why do you think they chose the church they did?

From my studies, there are only three reasons nonchurch people (or even newly relocated church people) decide to visit a specific church.

1. Denomination. A visitor comes because, even though they do not attend church, someone they knew was a certain denomination or they have heard good things about the denomination. That sounds simplified, but denomination tells people volumes about your church. In some parts of the country it's great to be a Lutheran church; in others, it's Baptist all the way; and in others, Assemblies of God are the ones to attend. Is your church's denomination name (or lack thereof) an asset or a hindrance in your neighborhood?

2. Relationship. Visitors come because they have confidence in someone who attends or has recommended the church. Evaluate your congregation for a second. Your church members are walking billboards. If they shine while talking about your church or if other believers in your community think your church is doing it right, you will be drawing people and that translates into uninvited visits. In the next section we will talk about how to empower these influencers as assets in church growth.

3. Curb appeal. Visitors come because the church makes them feel invited either by convenience, architecture, signage, web presence, or through other PR/marketing efforts. If your church can make them feel comfortable by having architecture that matches their lifestyle, signage that relates to their aesthetics,

Is your church built to make visitors feel as if you thought of everything for them, or does it make them feel as if they are an afterthought—uninvited to the party?

or a sense of welcoming that gives them comfort, you have made great strides. The more you can make them feel that you are prepared for them before their visit (for example, a visitor-friendly website, exterior signage with information on service times, and a clear path to indicate where visitors are supposed to go), the more comfortable they feel about coming. Is your church built to make visitors feel as if you thought of everything for them (think back to the queen of Sheba), or does it make them feel as if they are an afterthought—uninvited to the party?

A natural reason many churches see growth is simply that they are the right denomination in the right part of town and have influential people sitting inside their welcoming buildings.

### Getting Your Current Members to Invite Friends

A client called after a number of meetings with his church board to advise that they had decided to launch a contemporary service. It was a large church—over five thousand—but had relied on traditional services to connect with a strong over-fifty population. After many years of debating the issue, they were finally ready to reach out to a younger crowd that had been growing for some time in the community around them but not in their church.

A name for the service had come up in their meeting—a name that had become somewhat common through its use in a number of high-profile churches. The name they had discussed was "The Gathering." Their board had taken it one step further and decided to call it "The Praise Gathering." Excited with the progress that had been made with the board, my client said he had the go-ahead to roll out a large campaign for a new service under this name.

I was a little perplexed. I knew how hard fought this was, but yet I knew their idea was half-baked. I asked the client to approach his board with the following scenario . . .

Imagine a young woman—let's call her Julie. Julie works in an office of about thirty-five people. She is a customer service rep handling business-to-business sales. She is in her early thirties and is a believer in Christ. In the cubical next to her sits Suzie. Suzie is quite the party girl. She is loud and boisterous about her fun. Every Monday she draws an office crowd by discussing her escapades from the weekend. She drinks and lives a promiscuous lifestyle. Julie has wanted to minister to Suzie for some time. She has sent uplifting emails and said encouraging things from time to time, but it has become apparent that Suzie has no real spiritual context—leaving Julie to assume that Suzie has had little or no exposure to church.

Julie is shy by nature. She knows that God has put her in the position to be a light to her office. She struggles to get up the nerve to invite Suzie to church. Do you think it will be easier for her to invite Suzie to "The Gathering" or to "The Praise Gathering"? Suzie likely does not know how to praise. She may feel intimidated or awkward at the suggestion. If it is easier for Julie to mention "The Gathering" to her friend, there is both a greater likelihood that Julie will ask and a greater likelihood that Suzie will feel less intimidated and respond positively.

My client friend got the picture and took it to the board. The board acquiesced. About three months later, after we had rolled out a full-blown campaign and community blitz, the church was seeing growth like it had not seen in decades. The pastor called me to share that "there were people inviting people to church that had not invited people in over ten years." The excitement was palpable. The name, the materials, the ministry team, and the membership were all aimed strategically together toward a common end.

By now, I bet a church in every major city has a service named "The Gathering." I am not advocating it as a cookie-cutter solution for your church. Here's the principle: the easier the invite, the more likely it will happen. Make it easier and less intimidating on all parties, and it will happen more often. Prepare for it internally, and it will create results and foster growth.

Let's take a deeper look at the second way new people attend church—accompanied by a churchgoer. In the section before, we discussed the intimidation factor for a lone visitor in a new church. It's huge. But it is nowhere close to the stress and vulnerability that is put on the inviter of a first-time visitor. All inviters put their reputations on the line every time they invite someone to church. You can rest assured that your church members will not invite someone if they do not expect a positive outcome. And most of the time, that's why your church *isn't* growing and the church around the corner *is*. Remember our saying from chapter 2, "People are not ashamed of Christ, they are ashamed of their church." Ouch again!

I asked a young friend how he was enjoying his church; he admitted that he loved it but was bothered by the fact that the church wasn't growing. I asked him why it wasn't growing; he acted bewildered and said, "I have no idea."

"Yes, you do," I challenged him. "You know why it's not growing."

After a silence, I asked, "When was the last time you invited someone?"

"Well, it's been a long time," he said ashamedly.

"Why don't you invite people?"

He shuffled his feet and said, "I don't know."

"Yes, you do," I said. "The reason you don't invite people is the same reason why your church is not growing."

I could tell that bells went off on the inside. He responded, "Yeah, I know why." He had known it all along. He just had never connected the dots between the challenges of inviting people and overall church growth.

It might be simple. A congregant might be embarrassed about the church decorations, the woman who shouts from the back of the church, or the pastor telling jokes about his wife. The harder it is to invite people, the more challenging church growth is.

You see, I knew my friend loved God and wanted others to experience Christ's love. Unfortunately, most people are not intimidated about being Christians; they are intimidated about inviting people to their church.

This brings up one of the foundations of premarketing and the springboard to church growth: the easy invite. If an invitation is hard to make, for whatever reason, fewer people will be invited. The battle for growth is first fought in the hearts of churchgoers who want to better the lives of those around them. This is actually the desire of the vast majority of churchgoers.

> The battle for growth is first fought in the hearts of churchgoers who want to better the lives of those around them.

I cannot say this emphatically enough—all true Christians want other people to become Christians. It is planted in them when Christ is planted in them. This means if your church is having to beg, push, cajole, offer incentives, or even just remind people in your membership to invite others, it is a telltale sign that, for whatever reason, they do not believe the ministry that takes place will make a successful connection with the people they would invite.

Even if your church members learn to become effective evangelists on a personal level—a goal of every church—they still have to assimilate their newly believing friends into church in order to see them grow in Christ. If they feel that there will be a disconnection, a member deals with the concern of seeing their converted friends fall short in their Christian walk. If there is limited connection, the member has to rely on the motive of obligation to kick in. Any believer would much rather their friends feel at home coming to church.

This is where the rubber hits the road. "Becoming as one to win one," "knowing your target markets," "lingering with the masses," "sitting in their seat," is where all of it really counts. Is your church connecting with your community? The main

> Is your church connecting with your community? The main link is through your congregation, and if they think you're not connecting, you won't.

link is through your congregation, and if they think you're not connecting, you won't.

It is no wonder Paul challenged us in advance to "become as one to win one." The ability to relate to our communities and church growth go hand in hand. When a ministry can successfully relate to the people in its congregation, the churchgoers will be willing to invite others because they know it will relate to those they invite.

The following are just a few common reasons for the disconnect that diminishes a church member's willingness to invite. These topics can be obstacles as well for your uninvited visitor. As a side note, my guess is that none of these topics would ever show up on a visitor survey. They require us to look closely in the mirror, as even our closest allies would have a hard time advising us of some of these issues.

### Obstacles to Hospitality

- Singling out visitors: Having visitors raise hands or asking them to speak (I swear I've seen this happen) could embarrass them.
- Assumption: Saying, "Let's start where we left off last week" assumes they were there. Blindly referring to a Bible story or character assumes everyone knows it.
- Poor direction: Little or no signage and no explanation/introduction of the church as a whole leaves visitors in the dark.
- Inside jokes: Hearing these just reminds visitors they are outsiders.
- Scolding: Challenging members on issues that visitors should not hear, such as not inviting enough visitors or not volunteering enough, isolates visitors.

- Poor delivery: In our media-saturated world, people are accustomed to seeing things done well. An unprofessional implementation of your message shows a lack of care that will not be lost on non-churchgoing visitors.

### Obstacles to Comfort and Compatibility

- Social differences: If the church is categorically different from the potential invitee to a point where discomfort is expected, an invitation or a return is less likely.
- Style and culture: If the church or a component (for example, the congregation, décor, worship, or minister) is decades ahead or behind or opposite of the visitor's lifestyle, there will be intimidation to invite or return.
- Attire: Awkwardness occurs if the visitor would not be able to wear or know to wear the appropriate attire to be consistent with the congregation.
- Organization: Unprofessionalism affects the ability to appeal to professional people.

### Obstacles to Consistency

- Unpredictability: If members are not completely secure as to what the ministry topics are or who the speaker will be, they cannot invite accordingly.
- Time frames: Variance in length of the service can pose obstacles to visitors' schedules or expectations.
- Different outcomes: Members may not be sure whether the service will end with clear spiritual direction or invitation.

### Obstacles to Relevance

- Life application: Visitors may be unable to find nuggets of value for their life.
- Topical connection: The topic discussed might have no bearing on a visitor's life.

- Spiritual depth: If complex spiritual truth cannot be applied by people at every spiritual level, visitors might leave with no practical application.
- Boring delivery: If visitors are not captivated, they probably won't return.
- Nothing life-changing: If there is no call to growth toward a new level, why go?

### Obstacles to Understanding

- Depth: If a fourth-grader cannot follow the sermon, a visitor won't be able to.
- Non-sequiturs: Stream of consciousness preaching may leave the message unfollowable.
- Vocabulary: Speaking in "Christianese," or words that have no meaning or different meaning outside of church, leaves visitors thoroughly confused (Eucharist, atonement, sacrificial covenant, anointing, grace, blood of Jesus, etc.).

### Obstacles to Sensitivity

- Too much too fast: Demanding seasoned-believer performance without proper context from a congregation that includes babes and upper-deckers confuses and frustrates.
- Inner-court stuff: If "eat my flesh" (remember when Jesus said this?) type ministry takes place without proper explanation, it makes it harder on visitors and potential visitors.
- Confusing stuff: If things uncommon to a visitor (hands, tongues, communion, etc.) take place without proper explanation, you run the risk of alienating.

These are just some of the common obstacles to church growth. They apply to the uninvited visitor, the invited visitor, and the person considering whether he or she wants to risk the only chance he or she may have to connect a friend to church.

By analyzing the temptations and challenges associated with inviting people to church, we found the following to be true. If a churchgoer can answer these six questions positively, then inviting friends and family will not only be easy, it will become a lifestyle. The church will explode with growth!

*1. Will my friend feel welcomed?*

Hospitality—The atmosphere, nomenclature, and style of service should be inviting and not intimidating to the unchurched.

*2. Will my friend fit in?*

Comfort and Compatibility—Like it or not, invitations and visitor comfort decrease when cultural gaps exist.

*3. Can I feel confident that I know how the service will turn out?*

Consistency—People need to know what to expect, because they will invite accordingly.

*4. Will my friend get something out of it?*

Relevance—The message should be relevant and powerful for people at all spiritual levels.

*5. Will my friend understand it?*

Understanding—Jesus taught through practical illustrations. The songs and message should be understandable for people at all spiritual levels.

*6. Will anything that could seem strange to the unchurched be explained through Scripture?*

Sensitivity—Scriptural actions should be carried out with clarity and considerate explanation.

## The Value of Value

What is value? I do not mean in the sense of "a good deal," but in the sense that the church service or a component thereof distinguishably enhanced someone's life. If your church is having a difficult time getting people to come to your Sunday night service, think about its perceived value. This does not excuse people from being apathetic; it just gives us insight to consider if there are things we can do to the service to increase its value in the lives of people. If they are not coming, they do not think it is valuable in light of alternatives. The goal for Sunday morning: make your service more valuable to them than being home for the kickoff at noon. Increase what is put into it in a relevant fashion and you increase its worth in the lives of your congregation. Increase its value and people will feel they are missing something if they stay at home.

The number of visitors that attend as a result of member invitations is a primary way to determine the connectedness of your church. It is a measure of how valuable they feel the service will be in the lives of others. In most cases, it gives you insight into what your church members are not telling you directly. In some cases, you might find people who are avid inviters but never seem to get people to stick. The second litmus test for determining how well your church is connecting with the outside world is visitor retention. Look at the votes cast or not cast by visitor returns. Would you like to know how you're doing with uninvited visitors? Simple. Look at your visitor cards and count them. How many uninvited visits do you have per week, per month, per year? How many visitors return and become members?

You can learn a lot about how well your church is connecting with your community by how many visitors return. As an illustration, if I owned a restaurant where less than 20 percent of the people who visited ever returned, you would tell me I needed to fire the chef, get a new menu, or replace the wait staff. Unreturning visitors in commerce and in church are a sign that there is a disconnection somewhere. There are a million reasons they might not return but only one reason they do—value. And the more applicable and life-changing the service is to them, the more valuable they will find it. The higher the value, the more likely they will

> You can learn a lot about how well your church is connecting with your community by how many visitors return.

return. If they didn't find it valuable, you might have missed your chance—pray you catch them on the follow-up or that they find value at another church. This is even the case with lower-deckers and those on the field. By their actions, people vote on what they feel is valuable.

Now, don't get me wrong; value might be the members' or visitors' problem. Their values might not be in proper order and that is not to be overlooked. It does, however, make sense to say that raising the level of value a church creates will increase the number of people who find it more valuable than their alternatives. Thus, we cannot be successful obligating people to things if we do not take the time to do them well.

Ultimately, value is a combination of consistency, relevance, and power. Notice I include power. I believe we should be simple enough to be understood yet powerful enough to change lives. Provide services on visitors' level and do it consistently, and they will return and return with friends.

## Moving Forward

Most of what stymies church growth relates to these fundamental issues. Be honest. Diagnose it. Pray over it. Be willing to change. Know where growth comes from. Church growth is enhanced by prayer, but it is not mystical. New people do not fall from the sky. Growth comes from people showing up on their own and from people bringing people. It comes laterally from other churches or other communities or it comes vertically by spiritual conversion.

The bottom line is that it comes from connecting well with visitors. If you don't connect well, they won't return, and your people will be more hesitant to invite. Church members learn this and invite less and less. Do not count on the second-chance visitor. I remember consulting for a church where we reported that the ministry was extremely deep and complex. One needed a degree in theology to fully appreciate it. The leadership responded by sending me three CDs and saying, "Listen to these sermons; they are more like what we usually share." I asked them if they did that for all their visitors. Typically, you get only one chance to connect.

Take a moment to think again about uninvited visitors. Think of their challenges. As a church, have you done everything you can to remove speed bumps from their ability to receive the knowledge of Christ? Are they well directed? Would the congregation make them feel at home? The worship? The ministry? If you do not take their feelings into consideration, you likely will not get them to hear the message or to return. Then you have a better chance of growing only by way of lateral growth.

Think about the members. They want to invite people. What are the obstacles that keep them from feeling comfortable about inviting specific people? Write them down.

How could your church be more welcoming to visitors?

How can you enhance your church's compatibility with your community?

Are your services inconsistent? How could they be more consistent and still keep things fresh?

How can your services be more relevant to people at all spiritual levels?

How could every aspect of the service be made relatable to all levels of understanding?

Is your church sensitive? What can you do to ensure that you provide more answers and provoke fewer unanswered questions?

Think about value. Is it consistent? Is it relevant? Is it powerful? Write down what you can do to make the experience more valuable for each visitor.

Chapter 6

Setting the Atmospherostat • Ministry from the Outside In • Spiritual
Signposts • Creating a Ministry Pattern • Moving Forward

# Creating an Atmosphere
# That Fosters Growth

There is an entertaining video seminar used by a number of accounting firms across the globe to educate small business owners on how to be successful. It is called "Making Your Business Really Fly." Some of its thoughts are reminiscent of stellar, timeless business books like *Good to Great* by Jim Collins and *The e-Myth* by Michael E. Gerber. It is a truly engaging video seminar starring an Australian pet shop owner affectionately referred to as "Wally." Wally gives an example in the course of his teaching that bears repeating.[1]

Sitting down with his business advisor friend, Wally begins to tell a story that provides a valuable lesson. The story is inspiring and encouraging. For ten minutes or more, Wally paints a vivid picture and literally holds his friend's hand through the story—which has the effect of deepening their understanding of the subject and one another.

Wally engaged his friend in the lesson and made sure he was fully appreciating its worth. After Wally completed the story, he reared back and slapped his friend in the face. Stunned, his business friend was overwhelmed with pain and shock. Once his friend came to, Wally asked him, "Do you remember what we were talking about in the story?" His friend answered, "All I remember is that you slapped me in the face!"

Wally used this example to show businesses that oftentimes we do something to a client that is the equivalent to a slap in the face and that when it happens, the client forgets everything else—even the good that happened before the slap. I bring up this example because it is applicable to church growth.

A slap in the face to a visitor can be a number of things. It can be an insensitive comment from the pulpit, a moment of awkwardness, a harsh word from an usher, a haughty glance from a member, an "unnatural display of spirituality," or a rebuke levied at the congregation. Whatever it is, it can leave visitors reeling, forgetting everything good they might have heard.

Some churches even encourage behavior that has shocking effects on the visitor. No matter how spiritual it seems, Paul taught us to be sensitive to what visitors might think. Let's look at 1 Corinthians 14. Paul builds the entire chapter up to get us to see what a visitor might think of our church. He even encourages the Corinthians to pursue certain spiritual gifts over others as it was important that if "there come in those who are uninformed or unbelievers, will they not say that you are out of your mind?" (1 Cor. 14:23). Paul was once again concerned about what the visitor will think. He had growth savvy. His commitment to "Let all things be done decently and in order" (1 Cor. 14:40), was an attempt to keep visitors from getting emotionally slapped in the face with something that made no sense to them.

> In 1 Corinthians 14:23, Paul was once again concerned about what the visitor will think.

There are other ways the unchurched get slapped in the face. I have heard a pastor levy a rebuke so hard the walls shook. I have seen greeters slight visitors who did not fit in. I have heard ministers degrade their spouses from the pulpit. I have heard children's workers scream harshly at children. In reality, any severe violation of the six questions we learned from the previous chapter has the equivalent effect of a slap in the face.

Case in point . . . it was the largest church in a small blue-collar town. It had been a church of fifteen hundred in an area of perhaps sixty thousand. The church called us when they shrank to about eight hundred. They could not see what was causing the reduction. The pastoral staff had become accustomed to being the largest church in town. They had been successful in their own right. They had begun traveling and ministering in some of the churches we call "mega." Over the years, the staff's attire changed. In a town where the nicest store was JCPenney, they began to wear $2500 suits—and flashy ones at that. Makeup increased beyond community standards as did style of hair. The disconnect with the factory worker was more and more obvious—to the factory worker, that is.

It was a clear violation of question 2: will my friend fit in? Paul would become as a blue-collar worker to win one. That does not mean we do not look nice, but if you called a staff meeting and everyone was wearing button-down shirts and khakis and I showed up in a tuxedo, you might not think I was on the same page as you. The ministry leaders challenged my finding, claiming, "This is who we are; no one is offended by how we dress." A young music minister began to cry. He spoke up. "When I first came to this church, my wife and I lived four months with our cousins because we were so ashamed of our clothes compared to yours; we spent four months of our rent money to try to buy clothes to fit in with you."

Most of the team got it, but one of the leaders was still defiant. "This is me. This is how I like to dress. This is me!" she said.

Brother or sister in Christ, it is not about you and me; it is not about them. It is about the lost. If, by becoming more like them we are able to win one, is it not worth it? I am happy to say this last leader finally got it. An atmosphere that fosters growth is an accommodating one, not a self-focused one.

Just like removing a knife from the wound is the first step in starting the body's natural process of healing, removing these disconnections is the first step in jump-starting church growth.

> Just like removing a knife from the wound is the first step in starting the body's natural process of healing, removing these disconnections is the first step in jump-starting church growth.

Our six questions are the foundation for invitations and therefore the foundation for growth. 1. Will my friend feel welcomed? 2. Will my friend fit in? 3. Can I feel confident that I know how the service will turn out? 4. Will my friend get something out of it? 5. Will my friend understand it? 6. Will anything that could seem strange to the unchurched be explained through Scripture?

When you score high in these areas, the atmosphere within the church begins to take on a new feeling. When coupled with clear vision, your church gains new vigor. Did you ever notice, back when you were in high school, that when a guy did not have a girlfriend, no one wanted to date him, but the moment he had a girlfriend, all the other girls took interest? It is an air of confidence that attracts—a synergy that gives you wings. The "girlfriend principle" is alive and well in churches today. It starts with the atmosphere you create.

Atmosphere—what does that have to do with church growth? Many will think the very suggestion is an attempt to devalue the work of the Holy Spirit and the power of prayer, but it is completely the opposite. The fundamental component of any church's atmosphere is the sense that God is among His people and is active in their lives.

Remember, the Bible says that Peter and John were clearly "perceived" as "uneducated and untrained men," yet the onlookers "marveled" at their "boldness"—"And they realized that they *had been with Jesus*" (Acts 4:13, emphasis mine).

They had a powerful spiritual walk that was evident. It created an atmosphere around them. People must be able to recognize that a church's leaders and members have been with Christ and that His Spirit is active in the church. If it is not recognizable, the church will have a hard time making an ounce of difference in people's lives. It is the cornerstone of the atmosphere you create. The other major factors that contribute to atmosphere—like we saw with the example of the queen of Sheba—must be built upon it.

As we consider and analyze these facets, please know there are no universal fixes to every challenge. There is no secret formula for your church to become perfect. Your church worships differently, ministers differently, and has personality and doctrinal differences from churches around you. As I work with churches, I have seen a number of challenges created by churches following another church's model with expectations of similar results. Remember, methods are not universal—principles are.

Glean from others the principles, rather than the methods, that have helped them grow. There is safety in a "multitude of counselors" (Prov. 11:14), but there is no protection for a multitude of imitators. The internal and external dynamics that surround a growing church are so unique; you simply cannot do what Church X did and get the same results. Your church is not Church X. You do not have their members, their minister, their building, their community, or their staff. You cannot copy a method to create the right experience; it must be a result of the synergy of who you are as a church and the people you are trying to reach. There is simply no getting out of our need to "become as one to win one" and "linger with the masses" in our communities. Those are principles, not methods.

## Setting the Atmospherostat

Every church has an atmosphere. Atmosphere is the "dominant intellectual or emotional environment or attitude" of your church (according to Webster). Not every visitor can tell you in plain English what atmosphere they experienced, but every church has one—or more.

Ministry tone plays a big part. The music ministry plays a large part. So do architecture, environmental graphics, and lighting. So do ushers, teachers, and so on. Every church creates an atmosphere—some do it deliberately and some never stop to think what they are showing those people who "look on the outside."

In this section, let's start thinking about the atmosphere we create. Think about the experience we are currently giving our congregation and our visitors. Think about how we do things and what it says to the people around us. The current atmosphere might not be ideal, but it's imperative to understand that we completely control the atmosphere in our churches.

If you want to change the atmosphere, just like setting your thermostat, you have to adjust the internal cultural and communication habits of your team. You set the atmosphere. Set a mark and rise to it by inspiring, teaching, and training your leadership and church.

Recently I was sitting in my local Starbucks and overheard a group training session for new employees. It was great! Everyone was being trained on the atmosphere and experience they were being hired to create. The mission statement and core tenets painted a picture. Practical application was given through examples so everyone could grasp it. The meeting was defined—it was visionary. It was team building and it was exciting. I almost filled out an employment application.

I noticed that the Starbucks trainers had a vision (fancy word for a picture) of how employees should treat each other, their leadership, and their co-workers. Yet, their tone was not centered around what the workers wanted to get out of work. It was centered around an experience they would provide for one another and ultimately for their guests. Trainees were being taught to be relational with frequent customers and to be sensitive to those who did not know what a latte was. I sat there thinking about Nehemiah when he set his team in order and gave them individual job responsibilities as well as team strategies in the job of rebuilding Jerusalem (Nehemiah 3–4).

What if our churches put this much effort into instilling workers—volunteers and members—with a vision for the spirit of the church they would be part of and the atmosphere they would create for visitors? Without this vision, is it any wonder why we often come across as so fragmented and ineffectual to the people we are trying to reach? Is it any wonder why there are so many churches connecting with so few people? So far in the book we have discussed how little we know about the people we are trying to reach—what might be worse is that we often know very little about who we are.

Let's embark on this process of determining our atmosphere and then setting our *atmospherostat* (I know, I made it up) higher.

Since we have determined that church growth is largely the by-product of church members inviting friends and family, it is crucial that we think about how atmosphere affects both the churchgoers and the visitors. Ultimately, we want to set the stage for the experience to the upper deck, the lower deck, and the playing field. Let's then endeavor to determine the components of a rewarding church experience—components that engage the visitor, give the inviter the confidence needed to "compel them to come in" (Luke 14:23), and also challenge the seasoned believer.

By now, we should have done a bit of introspection, along with some analysis of our community. This is where those elements intersect. Think about where the core of your target community sits on Maslow's Hierarchy of Needs. Think about people's lifestyles, their income, how they interact in the workplace.

Picture Visitor Vic. He has lived in the community for many years and makes about 25 percent more per year than your average church member. He is a leader and people value his opinions. He also is not a churchgoer. He hasn't been since he was six, but he has some hidden challenges that have made him think about returning to church. What will he think about your church?

To help us analyze, let's look back at the principles behind the six questions from the last chapter: hospitable (welcoming), comfortable (or culturally connecting), consistent, relevant, understandable, and sensitive. If I were using them in evaluating my church experience or atmosphere, I would start on the outside and ask, "To a visitor, is my church name established on each of those principles?" You might run into some snags if your

> Your church name alone can position you out of some people's consideration simply because if they do not understand it, they are likely to feel intimidated by it.

church is named the "Holy Temple of Apostolic Glory" in an upscale community. Your church name alone can position you out of some people's consideration simply because if they do not understand it, they are likely to feel intimidated by it. They wonder if they could make sense of what goes on inside the church if they don't understand what the name means.

In the same way, look at each major "atmosphere" factor and determine what signals you are sending in light of these six principles. For the following, rate yourself from a visitor's perspective on a scale of 1–10 for each principle: hospitable, comfortable, consistent, relevant, understandable, and sensitive. I'll do the first one to help you get started. Believe it or not, each of these aspects gives Vic impressions of the church. Each element builds on the others. Analyze the job each of these do in forming a strong connection with Vic. Rate each aspect (1–10) as to how well it connects with him in these areas.

- External promotion

    Rate how welcomed Vic would likely feel (hospitable)

    Rate how likely Vic would feel compatible with the church culture (comfortable)

    Rate how likely Vic would walk away knowing what a typical service is like (consistent)

    Rate how likely the message would have dealt with issues Vic recognizes in his life (relevant)

    Rate how likely Vic is to comprehend the message and terminology (understandable)

    Rate how likely Vic would not be made to feel awkward (sensitive)

- Church website
- Building architecture and grounds
- Parking lot aesthetics and signage
- Greeters

- Ushers
- Children's workers
- Foyer area aesthetics and signage
- Printed materials
- Interaction from the congregation
- Announcements
- The worship service
- The offering
- The message
- The wrap-up, challenge, or altar call
- The benediction
- The dismissal
- The exit from the parking lot

Once you've done that, write a sentence or two about each of these aspects—define how these would ideally look to Vic. Now what would happen if you took each of these fundamental aspects of your service and determined what you want people to walk away saying or thinking? What if you redecorated, redesigned, taught, and trained until your atmosphere, communication, and your people all were aimed toward the same predetermined experience for the visitor? Your team has the ability to control the atmosphere. The better you know the people who are visiting, the more successful you will be in setting the atmosphere to help foster a life-changing experience.

Having a vision for a predetermined atmosphere or experience is quite bold. One of the core challenges to such planning is that it takes tremendous sensitivity and vision. It takes commitment. It takes the willingness to say, "This is who we are and this is who we are not." It takes truly understanding your current and desired connection with your members and your community.

Since the church experience is such a dramatic factor in church growth, we always pound away at it in the course of our consulting sessions. I have seen ministry teams pick it up and run with it to yield results that shifted growth from a standstill to 25 percent within about six months. I have also seen ministries sit completely still—changing nothing—yielding nothing. Ultimately, a good plan is only as good as its follow-through. A good sense of desired atmosphere is only as good as your willingness to continually track and adjust.

## Ministry from the Outside In

You might ask why I suggest putting so much stock in the visitor experience. Remember our baseball example? We categorized people as disconnected outside the ballpark, evaluating in the upper decks, committed in the lower deck, and dedicated on the playing field. By maximizing the experience for the upper deck, we enhance everyone's ability to bring a friend along. After all, if there were no $2 nosebleed tickets, how many new people would ever get introduced to the game?

Many churches actually create the atmosphere for the lower-deckers and players. Why? We, as leaders, hear their cheers the loudest. These lower-deckers and players are paying more for their seats. This is not to suggest that most churches even recognize this, but really, many churches' messages only have applications for the players and the lower deck. Much of the time when we consult with churches, we find the Sunday morning service would be lost on an unchurched person. This atmosphere keeps lower-deckers and players from inviting upper-deckers, because they recognize the likely disconnect that will exist. Now don't forget, churches can grow by focusing the experience toward lower-deckers—they just grow laterally, gaining ground from other churches, not from the community of unchurched.

One of the common concerns churches have with ministering to all levels is that, in theory, they feel it requires watering down the message. That simply is not the case. A strong church must have ministry that is focused on the lower-deckers and the players on the field—it is a matter of spiritual growth. Paul even makes a point for the need to move from the "milk" to the "solid food" of God's Word (1 Cor. 3:2). It probably sounds like a contradiction, but it is possible to minister well to upper-deckers, lower-deckers, and players, even in the same service. You just have to remember to pass out milk and meat in the same service. And while you're at it, make sure you pass out the milk first.

How do you do that? It does come easier for some ministers than for others. Ministers who are involved in evangelism on a personal level or frequent "lingering with the masses" often have a leg up on communicating to people across all levels. It's really like working a muscle. The ability to communicate with the lost in a service is strengthened through situations that require spiritual sensitivity on a personal level. If that does not come across naturally, a good way to frame your communication is to minister from the outside inward. I admit, this is part "method," but it is strong in principle. Ministry from the outside in suggests that you take a message and contextualize and deliver it for the upper deck first, then to the lower deck, and then to the players. Here's an example.

I was in a large church's regular Sunday service that turned into a volunteer drive. The minister spoke on "purpose" as an inroad to explain the need to serve in the local church. His message sounded like this:

> Every one of you has been given a purpose by God. You can find that purpose by giving of yourself. We are in such great need for volunteers; I pray you will see that unlocking your purpose starts by giving of your time to volunteer. Every single one of you needs to be working in the church. I challenge you to get involved this month.

When he rounded the corner to say, "Every single one of you needs to be volunteering in the church," I knew he thought he was only talking to the players and his lower deck. He would have never said that face-to-face to a first-time visitor. But, in reality, there were more than twenty visitors that morning who were recipients of this challenge to teach a class, change diapers, and clean the church by the end of the month. As an unchurched visitor, I would have felt anywhere from annoyed to violated. I might be thinking that I wasted my Sunday morning to hear that. Or that you are telling me my value is not in who I am but in what I can do for the church. It might have even served to convince me that churches are only out to take from people—diminishing my likelihood of returning.

What's worse, all the regulars were thinking, "I'm glad I did not bring a friend this morning." If this type of message happens too often, people stop inviting people altogether.

Let's look at that same message delivered but contextualized to the understanding of an upper-decker first. It could go something like this:

> I'm glad you are all here this morning. Today we are talking about purpose. First off, if church is new for you, I want you to know that God has a special plan for your life. He loves you very much. The step God desires that you take is to get to know Him—to begin a relationship with Him. Toward the end of the service, we will provide you with some ways to do just that. Today, I am going to be challenging our members, our "regulars," those who have committed themselves to being a vital part of this church. Every one of you has been given a purpose by God. You can find that purpose by giving of yourself. We are in such great need for volunteers; I pray you will see that unlocking your purpose starts by giving of your time to volunteer. Every single one of you needs to be volunteering in the church. I challenge you to get involved this month.

Notice that the same message got preached? Not even a word of the message for the "regular" had to be changed. What happened is that the message was prefaced and contextualized for the upper-deckers. They knew early on what they needed to consider, that the bulk of the message was categorically not meant to browbeat them. The irony is that a few months after this consult, this same thing was happening in another church across the country. One of my wife's friends for whom we have been praying visited a church near her home for the first time in decades. She called us after her visit and said, "The preacher told us we all had to work in the nursery. I'm not ready for that; I just wanted to know more about God. I don't understand."

We must consider people at all levels. If we minister to the outsider first, it gives them context to understand what is being asked of the membership and not of them. This message could have gone even deeper. If the minister had wanted to challenge those currently working to work more, he could have contextualized that with the lower-deckers.

> Many of you are volunteering already. What you do is so valuable to the kingdom. I want you to pray about stepping out and serving more.

I'm not a trained preacher; I'm a marketer. My job consists of helping people be effective in managing perception as a means to connect people with their product. I am sure you can come up with a number of additional ways to communicate this effectively. Understand that, fundamentally, you always need to provide as much context as possible first to the people who have the least. Breaking down your challenges to address the different levels of involvement helps everyone in your congregation to understand their place in the church as well as their current challenge. And always keep in mind that the more you help a visitor understand, the more your regulars will feel comfortable about inviting them.

I would use the same principle in a nonchurch environment. Say I was an aerobics instructor who held regular classes and wanted to see growth. I know people visit the class because they want to better their lives. Some come from a workout background and others do not. I would start my class by explaining all the aspects and communicating that beginners should not feel obligated to overdo. I would let them know they are welcomed and should join in at their own pace. I wouldn't just yell to everyone that they are not doing a good enough job. I want people to move up to the highest level, but one step at a time.

Jesus started with ministry to those on the outside and ended in ministry with those who had the deepest knowledge of Him.

That is how Jesus managed it. Remember His ministry with the five thousand, the followers, and then His inner court (John 6). He started with ministry to those on the outside and ended in ministry with those who had the deepest knowledge of Him.

Since this is a method where the principle lies in sensitivity and relevance, you do have alternatives. You could create completely separate venues for people of different spiritual levels—the church equivalent of having beginner, advanced, and expert aerobics classes. This is completely viable for some; I'll give an example of it later in the chapter. However your church manages it, the end result should be ministry that has some application for everyone.

Still wondering if prefacing to whom you are communicating has merit? Paul did it. Paul prefaced his letter to the Ephesians: "Paul, an apostle of Jesus Christ by the will of God, To the *saints who are in Ephesus, and faithful in Christ Jesus*: Grace to you and peace from God our Father and the Lord Jesus Christ" (Eph. 1:1–2, emphasis mine). He had done much evangelism there, but this letter was specifically for the believers. He wanted to make that clear, because he would inspire and challenge them on things above the level of a nonbeliever.

When you start to put this into practice, the only grief you might catch will be from those "lifers" who are proud of their commitment to the lower deck and demand that the focus only be on ministry for them. Don't worry; they don't invite people anyway.

## Spiritual Signposts

My wife and I recently took a cruise and were amazed at how elaborate these vessels are. I could not imagine attempting to make it around the ship without a map. There were fourteen levels and infinite sections and activities. I wondered how many passengers might have made it to their room yet never saw the hundreds of activities that were available to them.

Do you ever wish you just had a map for your life? One of those nice big bulletin-board-sized maps with the nice big red dot that says, "You are here." If we had such a map, we would all do a better job of fulfilling our destiny. The challenge is that as we walk a walk of faith, the only sense of where we are comes from seeing ourselves in the mirror of God's Word (James 1:23) and from those God gives us to encourage and speak truth into our lives (Ephesians 1, for example).

This brings up two things that visitors suffer when attending a new church the first few times. They seldom are introduced to all the "ship" has to offer and even if they are, they have no context to understand where they are and what the next steps are for getting around the ship. They might experience only one room and assume they have seen it all.

What if we offered them a map? What if they could see where they were spiritually in the context of where they could be? What if, in every service, everyone was confronted with spiritual signposts that helped them see what progress looked like in their spiritual walk?

Most churches have different stages by which they categorize people. You might say the level of progression for your church is . . .

> What if, in every service, everyone was confronted with spiritual signposts that helped them see what progress looked like in their spiritual walk?

- Attendance
- Salvation experience
- Growth groups
- Membership
- Leadership class
- Volunteering
- Full-time staff

Whatever the steps are called, it is very likely that your staff knows what they are. It is also likely that many in your congregation have no idea what these steps are or their order. As many times as these steps are the topic of staff meetings, they are rarely communicated as directly to people during the service. Most regular churchgoers simply do not know.

If visitors and regulars alike were challenged to understand that they are attending and the next step in spiritual growth is the salvation experience, more would take the next step. People get bored of just going. People need to be constantly reminded where they are and what the next level is. Again, you might have a different set of signposts, but communicating them is only the beginning of seeing people grow spiritually in context with your church.

Without these signposts, people often visit a church and assume there is no next step; they either keep coming back or they don't. They do not inherently see what else is on the ship—the various levels and the different activities. By communicating it to them consistently, you enhance your ability to connect with them and see fruit borne in their lives.

The principle of what I am advocating here is not about a literal map (although you might find that helpful). It is found in the routine explanation of the scope of the ship and in a continuing effort of reminding people how to identify where they are.

For example, "Many of you who are here this morning might be checking this church thing out. I just want to challenge you to take the first step in beginning a relationship with God—that is, asking Christ to forgive you of your sins and become your Lord. Others here have made that commitment, and I challenge them to take the next step by returning to church and beginning to fellowship with other Christians. From there begin to . . ."

When you lay it out, you help people identify what level they are on and show them the next step. Remember Paul doing this in Acts? He used spiritual signposts to clarify where the Corinthians were in their walk. He asked them if they had received the baptism into Christ. They said they had only received the baptism of John (Acts 19:1–5). By helping them understand which signpost they were standing by, Paul was able to lead them into making Christ their Lord. Aquila and Priscilla had done the same with Apollos in the previous chapter (Acts 18:25–27). Think what great clarity comes from helping people understand where they are in the process of their spiritual walk.

As well, think of how valuable classifying the steps in spiritual growth is in evaluating ministry effectiveness. Simply look at the numbers of people engaged at every signpost level. These numbers are critical. The percentage of people who know about your church feeds into the number who attend, which feeds into the number who return, which feeds into the number who get plugged in, which feeds into the number who serve in ministry, which provides the support for what you need to do to grow. Notice the areas of the baseball illustration: those outside the ballpark, the upper-deckers, lower-deckers, and players on the field.

It works like a funnel. If your church is short on helpers, you probably have a clog somewhere in the pipe. The level of commitment required to move from one level to another also has an effect on the pass-through to deeper levels. If a low level of commitment is required, you will have a larger crowd but risk trivializing the responsibilities of spiritual maturity that come with

> The level of commitment required to move from one level to another also has an effect on the pass-through to deeper levels.

service. On the other hand, if your required commitment level is too high, you might be like some churches that have only four volunteers who hold up the weight of the entire church, expecting visitors to make it to spiritual maturity much too fast. I have seen churches that were not growing because the perceived standards (or the feeling that was left) were that perfection is required of every believer no matter how long he or she had known Christ. This creates such a black-and-white divide that grace is often overlooked and a perceived inner circle becomes an obstacle.

If your church does not have its signposts clarified, I challenge you to come together and define them now. Make it a part of every service to communicate them. Make a video or a graphical representation if needed to help illustrate the signposts.

### Creating a Ministry Pattern

When I served as a volunteer youth leader many years ago, I had the luxury of breaking the areas of ministry into specific segments. I had my "beginner," "advanced," and "expert" classes. On Friday nights, we offered a youth outreach where our warehouse was used as a backdrop for fun, games, and music. I would wrap up a night of fun with a fifteen-minute chat about what God had done in my life. I gave the youth the opportunity to make decisions for Christ; many did. I then challenged those who had given their lives to Christ to take the next step: "Come on Wednesday nights where you will learn how to walk with God." On Wednesday night they would get this invitation: "If you have been walking with God and He is compelling you to take your walk to the next level, I want to challenge you to come on Sunday nights where we will train you to be a student leader."

This is an example of how you can create multiple services to reach multiple levels. You do not have to do it this way, but it's an option for some. Either in separate services, by ministering in one service on different levels, or by creating a ministry pattern, you give members added confidence that you will connect with the visitors they bring, no matter what level they are at spiritually.

In our case we had a specific goal for each target audience. For the Friday night upper-deckers, our goal was to inspire them to see God for who He really was. On Wednesday night, we purposed to teach them how to walk with Christ. On Sunday night we were committed to train those who had a heart for ministry. Inspire. Teach. Train. That was our pattern. Teens knew it and invited people accordingly. If they wanted to invite a person at any spiritual level, they could judge for themselves which service would minister to them the best and invite accordingly. People will always invite according to what they think is going to happen. That's why changing speakers, changing topics, and even changing worship styles at the last minute can have a tragic effect on people who have invited friends. They often have worked months on getting this person there and purposefully invited them because they expected a connection with that minister, that topic, or even that worship style.

I'll never forget one Wednesday night when I realized that there were no visitors in our youth group and decided to do things a little differently. I had the girls and guys get into separate circles and asked them to take turns praying for the person to their right, going around the circle until all had prayed. At the time, I knew this was not protocol, but it sounded like a good idea. I knew who was there, and the prayer time, as expected, went just fine.

We proceeded with the service, and at its conclusion, a young teen girl came to me and asked, "Are we going to do that prayer thing every time? The reason I ask is because I wanted to invite a friend and I know that she would have felt horrible if she was asked to pray out loud for someone else. I'm not even sure she's a Christian."

I saw the fear on her face. She wanted to invite people, but now she was gun-shy. I immediately realized what I had done.

Without thinking, I had violated her trust in how the service would turn out. I jumped onto a couch and asked for everyone's attention as they were walking to the door. "I want everyone to know this. The fact that we did this prayer tonight was because I knew everyone here and I knew you could handle it. I want you to know that I will never put anyone you invite into a situation where they feel singled out or awkward. I'm sorry if I confused anyone, but I want you to know you can always invite friends and be confident that we will not do anything that will freak them out."

Several other kids thanked me for saying that because they too had been concerned about inviting friends as a result of this simple prayer time. This ties into one of our six principles—consistency. If you are not consistent, you make people second-guess whether to invite people.

> If members walk out of your service saying, "I wish my unsaved friend had been here," they will start to think about inviting their friend.

Having said all this, I am convinced of one thing. If members walk out of your service saying, "I wish my unsaved friend had been here," they will start to think about inviting their friend. If a member walks out of your service three weeks in a row and says every time, "I wish my unsaved friend would have heard that," nothing will stop that member from dragging that friend through your doors. The challenging thing is that often, when members walk out of churches, the only thing they can say is, "I wish my other church friends would have heard that." What we get as a result is only lateral growth.

## Moving Forward

Let's take a second to recap. Remember, as a church, you can set the atmospherostat. You also have to manage it. You can determine the experience people will have. You can decide what they will walk away saying about your church. The first step is defining it. Once you define your objective, you can evaluate all of your atmospheric elements in its light. Do that now.

Next, take a second to think about your signposts. Almost every church has them, but most churches keep them hidden. Signposts give direction and a path for growth. Without them, we cannot tell if we are making progress. How clear are they to you, your staff, your volunteers, your members, and your visitors? Are you overcommunicating them? If not, chances are you are undercommunicating them. Define them. Write them down. Make them plain and give light to spiritual growth.

Does your church's ministry start with the upper deck? Communicating to them and inspiring them early ensures that you connect with them and gives confidence to your members about inviting people. Write down some ways you can ensure you are connecting with those who are unchurched.

Are services consistent? The only churches that are successful by being inconsistent are those that grow laterally by exciting other church people. Consistency in a ministry pattern that challenges people to go from the level they are at now to the next level breeds confidence in your members. It ensures them they will never walk away apologizing to a visitor that the service was not what it sometimes is.

One last thing. What will you do to make sure that every service challenges the believers and also makes them walk away thinking, "I wish my unsaved friend would have been here"? If you make this happen, growth will never be a problem.

If you can work together to ensure these things, you have created the atmosphere for growth.

# Chapter 7

Students of Culture • Nailing the Perceived Need • Living in an Experiential World • Different Strokes (Segmentation) • Moving Forward

# Marketing Secrets of the Big Boys

By following Paul's example and studying God's Word as it relates to the most basic marketing principle—the management of perception—you can begin to establish where you are as a church. You can then adjust your actions and communications toward becoming who God has called your church to be. It takes understanding, planning, and practice to put it all together, but the principles behind perception management are universal. They are behind every advertising campaign you see. Billion-dollar companies utilize the same principles.

Imagine putting together a campaign without having first determined how your church is perceived, without studying your target audience, or without developing a strategic intent for your communications. The big boys don't do things that way. They realize there is too much at stake. They succeed or fail on the strategic accuracy of their managed perception. Most companies, large and small, take this very seriously. In almost every industry, spending on marketing (including research and advertising) is a minimum of 10 percent of a company's annual budget. Companies that focus on being on the cutting edge often spend as much as 20 percent of their budget on marketing. Could you imagine doing

> The big boys succeed or fail on the strategic accuracy of their managed perception.

that with your church? So why do those companies do it? Do you think they are spending carelessly? That's hard to imagine. For them, it's all about profit, and having learned that marketing helps them sell more, they see their marketing costs as an investment. Marketing is their leap of faith that they will connect with more profits.

Trends come and go. What excites me about a successful corporate marketing story is seeing how companies apply good principles to accomplish great things. Focusing on the ultimate course of action is kind of like reading David and Goliath just for the battle scene. The story means little unless you understand that David's boldness was born from his relationship with God.

## Students of Culture

When I think of the corporate application of lingering with the masses, I think of Mountain Dew when they helped usher in the extreme sports craze. Mountain Dew sponsored just about every skate park tournament across the country. If an activity could be considered outrageous, they were involved. Their advertising played on radical youth culture themes. "Done that! Did that! Been there! Tried that!" commercials ended in drinking "the Dew" to the tone of "Done it! Like it! Loved it!" The "Do the Dew" commercials helped establish the "wild man slacker" theme that summarized a generation. It was extremely profitable for them.

What I found most interesting is how their connection to this generation was fostered. Pepsico purchased the Dew brand in 1964 and saw relatively low sales for decades before they latched on to a rapidly developing social group that we have come to describe as Gen-X. In the early days, part of Pepsico's marketing research process created the foundation for their enduring brand.

Mountain Dew gained dramatic insight into the mind-set of a generation by lingering with the masses. They employed a team of college kids who put on Mountain Dew gear and went to local high school campuses in black Mountain Dew Hummers. They had several goals: (1) locate popular, trendsetting teens, (2) give them free stuff and invite them to hang out around the Hummer, and (3) take feverish notes on all they said, did, and wore.

Their ultimate goal: learn what the coolest kids in school called cool. Learn what was coming next in cool. Mountain Dew accomplished this by observing kids in an anthropological sense and learning from what they saw. This is how they caught on to the extreme sports craze very near its inception. They took particular notice of teens who they could tell were "early adopters" (marketing term for cutting-edge leaders or trendsetters). These teen influencers were the ones who were introducing clothing and hairstyles long before they became popular. It is one thing to observe people. Mountain Dew knew to observe the ones who were setting the trends. When you reach the leaders, you reach their followers. The trendsetters at the time had a common element that Mountain Dew used to create a powerful sense of belonging—that element: a respect for a lack of fear.

So how does this affect us in the church? Again, methods pass and brands pass, but the principle applies to how we can learn about the people we are called to connect with. If we listen to them and understand them, we learn better ways to relate to them. At our company, we have a slogan of "Changing the way the world looks at Christians." I believe we will accomplish that goal only if we start by "Changing the way Christians look at the world."

When you linger with the masses, do not expect them to come out and clearly say profound things about themselves. People do not normally talk in a straightforward manner about the real factors that control their decisions about life or church. You have to learn to interpret the data you receive. The practical lessons from the Mountain Dew story might be found in the following situations:

1. Your church reaches a lower-middle class demographic, but a middle to upper-middle class target audience is increasing in the community. Mingling with the masses might be as simple as having your leadership go out and play more golf. I'm serious. They shouldn't go out as a

group, of course, but have them fellowship individually with members of the target audience in a context in which those people are most comfortable. If you want to reach the country club class, you have to go where they are to learn where they are coming from. You may feel intimidated and awkward at first, but rest assured, when you feel more comfortable with them, you will gain insight on how to connect with them.

2. Your church is predominantly middle class and you desire to be more effective in ministry to a much lower class segment of your community. Lingering with the masses might mean several trips to the unemployment or welfare office to observe and to gain understanding of the process and the experience from the viewpoint of someone directly involved. It might mean spending time in stores you do not normally frequent just to gain a better understanding of their perspective. Or, at a greater depth of involvement, you might try having your family live on a frustratingly reduced budget for several months. When you've done all that, you can try to contextualize your church with their mind-set so that your marketing efforts can be geared to connect with the needs of your target audience.

> You will learn more about the people you are trying to reach by watching them in their element and understanding their underlying struggles and victories than you ever could by reading a book about cultural trends.

This approach is tremendously valuable in the biblical pursuit of becoming as one to win one. You will learn more about the people you are trying to reach by watching them in their element and understanding their underlying struggles and victories than you ever could by reading a book about cultural trends. Mountain Dew did not read the book. They wrote it, from experience.

## Nailing the Perceived Need

Remember our story from chapter 2 about the woman driving late at night needing gas to make it home? Which of two equally accessible gas stations would get her business? Our answer was that she would stop at the one with the better lighting. It's simple but truly profound. I imagine the owner of the less-frequented store dropping prices and scratching his head. "Why are we so slow at night when the other store is packed? Cutting prices doesn't work and increasing inventory hasn't increased sales. Redesigning the logo and a bigger advertising budget hasn't done it either."

The owner's disconnect here is about perceived needs. Sure, the late-night customer might want to save money some other time, but at that moment her most important need is safety.

Let's look at how the big boys handle perceived needs.

If you are old enough, you remember the early days of the running shoe market in the late seventies and early eighties. There were a number of new companies like Brooks, Puma, Saucony, Asics, New Balance, Adidas, and Pony. They were all competing against each other, all selling shoes that were pretty much alike. By the midnineties, Nike had established itself as the dominant player. How did Nike take over an entire market? Through brilliant marketing, Nike identified a perceived need that the others overlooked.

Nike sold us a perceived need—inspiration—but delivered our real need—belonging. Nike made us believe we could attain near superhuman achievement. How? By creating an indelible connection between their brand and Michael Jordan, a truly iconic figure in American sports. They created an identity behind the shoes by lining up top athlete endorsers from just about every sport. By the time Nike was telling us to "Just Do It," the company was already bigger than life. Theirs was a message of such simplicity that only Nike could get away with it. Why? Because they had primed us to see them as much more than just

> Nike
> inspired us
> to belong,
> yet they never
> asked us to belong.

footwear. They were the embodiment of what we could be, if we would "Just Do It." Nike inspired us to belong, yet they never asked us to belong. In public perception, they were, at the time, so linked to greatness that any other shoe was just "normal."

To buy Nike shoes was to be a part of something bigger than yourself. Nike was about belonging. We needed to belong; they sold it to us wrapped up in faith and achievement. Why do I think it was about belonging more than a true aspiration toward being better at sport? Because 90 percent of us never used Nikes for anything more athletic than going to the mall on Saturday. We did not want to run; we just wanted to belong to the winning team.

So what does this mean for a church?

For one, it helps us see the difference between true needs and felt needs. We all know the people we desire to reach need Christ. We can agree that God has given everyone an empty space in their heart that only He can fill. The challenge is, until they have heard and understood the message of redemption, many people likely cannot conclude their specific need for Him. They know they need to be in church or to have their kids in church. They feel there is something missing or they have questions in need of answers. We know the real, bottom-line need is belonging to Christ, but their perceived need is always something less spiritual.

Unless we can connect with people on the level they feel they need, we cannot introduce them to their real need.

Nike sold us belonging packaged in inspiration. Is there any other way to sell belonging? Do you think Nike would have been successful if they'd done a commercial without Jordan and *instead* used a slogan like "We make you feel like you belong"? It would have crashed and burned because people wouldn't have connected. Selling belonging overtly does not work.

You have to package it in something else—something great. Nike was able to draw deeply from almost every demographic by creating a sense of belonging to something bigger than life. They used inspiration. Inspiration knows no

Challenge me to go to the next level and no matter what level I am on, I will understand the calling.

boundaries. Challenge knows no boundaries. Challenge me to go to the next level and no matter what level I am on, I will understand the calling.

This means you never sell belonging by advertising it. Few people consciously think about an inherent need to belong. Most people only recognize it after they have filled it. If someone truly responded to a tag line like "A church where you belong," it would be the equivalent of answering an altar call without hearing a message. We know that belonging is a fundamental need, but one that is not generally acknowledged until it is fulfilled.

Back in the mid-1900s a new phenomenon swept over America. It was the birth of the gated community. As suburbs grew and new communities developed, it was common for a husband and wife to drive around an area looking for a new home. The trend that marketers picked up on is what I like to call the "in there" principle.

After looking at houses around all the communities, couples shared their likes and dislikes. With tremendous frequency, they would mention particular homes throughout the community, on this street and that street, but when they came across a subdivision that had a walled entrance, the wife especially would say, "I would like to live 'in there.'" The house might be identical to one just down the street, but the entry walls of the subdivision made all the difference. Outside the walls, people just lived "there." Inside the walls people lived "in there." The inclusion and belonging that "in there" created has literally shaped our landscape.

The inclusion and belonging that "in there" created has literally shaped our landscape.

This is just another example of the need for belonging playing out in our lives in a way that we would hardly notice. What this boils down to is that needs, such as Maslow's Hierarchy of Needs (food, safety, belonging, self-confidence, and self-actualization), are met inside the church but are not inherently tangible or perceived outside the church. Concepts more likely perceived are those that bring people from one level of need to another—such as inspiration. Find a way to inspire them and you'll give them a place to belong whether they knew the need existed or not.

## Living in an Experiential World

Another marketing dream—Starbucks. I think it inspires us so because the idea confounds us. We cannot believe we spend $4 on a cup of coffee, but we love to do it just the same. It is also one of the first examples of marketing and branding that we, as the church, seem to understand. Starbucks draws its strength by filling a social vacuum that was decades in the making—going all the way back to when few had air conditioners in their homes and families sat out on the front porch at night to keep cool and socialize. This is where community took place, where you knew your neighbors. That sense of community has been diminishing for decades. Starbucks is about rekindling that atmosphere as much or more as it is about coffee. Like Nike, Starbucks is fulfilling more than a need for coffee. They are filling our cups with caffeine, belonging, comfort, and community all at the same time.

Arthur Rubinfeld, former head of brand design for Starbucks, explained it this way: "You want a store located in the path of people's daily shopping experience, their route to work, on their way home from a movie. You want to be America's front porch, the place where people gather to meet neighbors and friends."[1]

To Starbucks founder and chairman Howard Schultz, there is even a higher call . . .

> Across all channels of American society and culture, there is such a fracturing of values. There are no heroes. . . . There is little trust in a number of public institutions. . . . I'm not saying Starbucks is going to save the world, because we can't . . . what we've done is provide a safe harbor for people to go. I think the brand equity of the name Starbucks has supplied a level of trust and confidence, not only in the product, in the trademark, but in the experience of what Starbucks is about. At a time where there are very few things that people have faith in. It's a very fragile thing. You can't take it for granted. It's something that has to be respected and continually built upon.[2]

A haven. A community center. So how do you go from coffee to haven? By creating a positive experience for the customer. "The most enduring competitive advantage we have is that we are able to give our customers a better experience at the store level . . . than any competitor we have out there," says Orin Smith, Starbucks CEO.[3]

In *The Experience Economy* by B. Joseph Pine and James H. Gilmore, the authors paint a brilliant picture of what makes us so addicted to Starbucks. At a fundamental level, coffee is a commodity, tradable by the ton in a commodities market. Starbucks wraps an experience around a cup of coffee, not unlike the atmosphere we talked about in the previous chapter or the one Solomon created in the temple. What makes Starbucks remarkable is that they did not create just any experience; they created a specific one. They created and mastered thousands of times over an atmosphere of stylish comfort. The colors of the flooring, the walls, the names for cup sizes, the staff that is trained to be your friend; it all adds up to the predetermined experience they want you to have.[4] Starbucks doesn't own the concept of experience, and they hardly invented it. They just brought it into our everyday lives. Experience has been a differentiating factor for big brands for years. Why stay in a Ritz-Carlton hotel? The experience. Why go to Disneyworld? The experience. Great companies set themselves apart by establishing the specific experience that identifies who they are. Urban Outfitters and Hollister Co. are not just clothing stores. A Mac is not just a computer. These items evoke great passion from the people that call themselves clients. They evoke a sense of pride—yes, a sense of belonging. There's a great line in the movie *You've Got Mail* that describes it. Joe Fox, the character played by Tom Hanks, says, "The whole purpose of places like Starbucks is for people with no decision-making ability whatsoever to make six decisions just to buy one cup of coffee. Short, tall, light, dark, caf, decaf, low-fat, non-fat, etc. So people who don't know what . . . they're doing or who on earth they are, can, for only $2.95, get not just a cup of coffee but an absolutely defining sense of self: Tall! Decaf! Cappuccino!"

In *The Experience Economy*, the authors reason that in the modern economy, companies create "experiences" to set themselves apart from "services." They explain that the trade of common goods progresses in stages, moving from commodities, to goods, to services, to experiences. In a classic example, they show how coffee went from being simply a commodity (something indistinguishable, mass-produced, and sold by the ton), to being a good or product (a packaged item for sale on a local level). If you would like to move beyond that so coffee makes it into a cup in front of you, with maybe some steamed milk and a flavoring, you're looking at a service. In order to thrive, a service must wrap an experience or atmosphere around it. Starbucks is their prime example. You do not buy coffee; you buy the Starbucks experience. You do not stay at the Westin, you lose yourself in the experience of a "Heavenly Bed."[5]

Some people might be offended by the suggestion that we consider the experience we create for the visitor on this level, but I think the greater crime is turning church into a commodity. A relationship with Christ cannot be canned. It cannot be mass-produced. It is an intimate and powerful thing and we should be very serious about enhancing the experience in order to prepare the heart of the visitor for the message. After all, would the queen of Sheba have been so receptive to Solomon had he surrounded himself with an unprofessional staff in a haphazard and ill-prepared setting? She was overwhelmed by the experience Solomon created. If companies work so hard to do this for coffee, why should churches settle for less when it comes to introducing people to Christ?

With that in mind, what do businessmen and women feel when, after developing successful, strategic companies, they step into a church that has just slapped things together or a church hiding behind a badge that it is "for the Lord"? Shouldn't there be even more thought in the concept and more care and excellence in the development if it is for God? Have you ever noticed how rarely you see those who embody corporate success in a tiny church? Why? The experience is too stressful. Who wants to come to church and see hundreds of ways to improve it, yet be burdened with the inability to help the leadership fathom or facilitate dynamic change?

> Who wants to come to church and see hundreds of ways to improve it, yet be burdened with the inability to help the leadership fathom or facilitate dynamic change?

Pine and Gilmore take the process one step further, to a level above experience. They call it transformation.[6] Interestingly these business experts point to ministry efforts such as Promise Keepers as entities that create transformation by combining an experience with life change. That is what our churches should be about. To get to transformation, you have to first create a defined and powerful experience. There are many churches that give service. There are some that provide an experience. There are even fewer that combine the experience with such a touch from God that it qualifies as a transformation. A transformation takes place when people are affected by the experience.

## Different Strokes (Segmentation)

If you were in a car accident and had what looked to be a fractured spinal column, whom would you prefer to visit? An orthopedic specialist or a general practitioner (family doctor)? I would want the orthopedic specialist. Why? Who wants someone with general knowledge when you can be treated by someone with specific expertise?

Have you ever been in a mall and noticed that when you see an Old Navy, you usually also see a Banana Republic and a Gap? Do you think that is a coincidence? It isn't. The Gap owns all three companies, and each has a different target audience. In general, Old Navy is the low-cost store that carries clothing "staples" for young people. The Gap carries more "fashion-forward" casual attire at a premium price. Banana Republic is an upper-scale line that caters to the modern yuppie (young urban professional)—clothes you can wear to work while still looking trendy. Ever wonder why they don't just put it all in one store? Because although each of the stores caters to younger people, they cater to very different young people. That is not to say that someone might not have clothes from each store, but it is obviously harder to consider paying Banana Republic prices ($85) for a shirt when it sits right next to an Old Navy sweater ($14.99).

America's greatest companies know the art and science of differentiation. Some companies, like Southwest Airlines, present themselves as "low-cost leaders." They proudly provide a basic good or service without frills or extras. Other companies represent options where the brand name itself commands a premium price, such as Louis Vuitton. Still other companies, such as Ralph Lauren, work to establish a classic cachet. Some struggle to identify who they are, like Luby's, known by many as the restaurant for the gray-haired, or like Target, which has become a hip version of Wal-Mart for the moderate middle class. The fact is, in a competitive world you have to give people a reason to choose you over their other choices. Very few can go head-to-head without taking a toll on one another.

In the same way, you can evaluate every church in your community. There are the ones with great worship, the ones with dwindling crowds, the ones with flashy preachers, the ones that preach hellfire and brimstone, and the ones with prestigious buildings. There is just about every kind of church you can imagine. Want to grow? Find out what kind of church people want and need and become that. If that already exists, your church will have to differentiate.

In the church world, our most common form of differentiation is called denomination. It allows someone to know almost everything about us in a word—Methodist. But that is no longer clear enough. Ministries who act outside of the "company line" increasingly muddle the clear distinction of denominations that once existed. Baptist might not mean Baptist like it used to. Churches are shedding denominational titles left and right. For someone contemplating a choice among churches, it is like stepping into a mall in which you do not recognize any of the store names. You have to step inside and ask, what kind of store are you? This creates its own set of challenges.

In preparing for a meeting with a church board, the pastor laughed and warned me, "The average age in our church is 126." I did not take that seriously until I showed up and saw that he was right! There was a man on the deacons' board that I prayed would make it through the meeting alive. I spoke of our services and how we could be of help to them. We had a nice meeting. Toward the end of our discussion the pastor challenged me. He said, "Our church building is 135 years old. Our congregation numbers about 400 and 70 percent of them are over 60 years old. We have not been able to reach the younger crowd. I am afraid if we make ourselves look fancy, people will visit but never return. That's just not who we are. What can we do to grow?"

The pastor also warned me that they were culturally and doctrinally very resistant to change from their traditional hymnals. He understood the challenge he was facing. What was seen as praise and worship to his generation is not recognized as such by the younger one—and vice versa.

My heart hurt for him. He was a man of passion and wisdom. I could see his concerns. I reassured him, "We have no intention of false advertising for you. What we will endeavor to do is connect who you are with those whom God has uniquely qualified you to reach. If you want to reach twenty- and thirty-year-olds there are a few obvious ways to do it, based on typical human nature. One, create an intimate men's Bible study that you lead. I will help you get it started. Base it on mentoring and pouring into the lives of a new generation. You are the kind of person young people flock to. You are approachable, heartwarming, and wise. After you work with these men in the small group setting, your challenge will be including them in your very traditional congregation."

The second option I mentioned was that he could hire a "pied piper," a young inspiring leader to develop a program for young adults. Even if the program were successful, though, the same problems would exist. How could he connect these young adults to a congregation with such a different lifestyle? And worse, if the connection didn't work, a successful young adults program may mean he would likely be looking at a church split in the future.

There was, however, a third option for the pastor. He could realize his weakness of being holistically an older generation church and make it his strength, using it as a springboard to reach out and evangelize the thousands of older citizens in the community who sit around on Sunday morning thinking, "I wish there was a church out there for me." These people may have had experiences with God at an early age but over the years have become separated from church. What if his church did a campaign to fulfill that need and reach into their lives? This church could value a generation that other churches are overlooking or not connecting with.

The pastor asked for a few days to think. When he called me, he said, "I like option three. We are who we are. I think we are going to embrace that and let our ability to connect with the older generation be used by God before they slip into eternity lost." He had new passion. He knew what his church was and whom they were called to reach. I would not dare question his decision; it was between him and God. I will, however, work with him to make him as effective as possible at connecting with the older people he feels called to reach.

Let's face it. Some churches are better at reaching young people. Some are better at reaching different ethnic groups. Some are better at reaching the affluent. Remember, your church is not the body. It is *part* of the body. Some churches are the eyes. Some are the teeth. Some are the fingers and others the toes. Is it fair to say that unless we are all things at once, we are not effective for the body? Learn to understand what part you are.

When I pass by my local Chinese Baptist church I do not think, "They should focus on the whole community and not just the Chinese." That's absurd. People will flock to where they feel comfortable and compatible. Some of the largest churches with the most diverse congregations have some of the smallest singles groups. Ever wonder why? People will never say it, but they have all kinds of hang-ups. They feel comfortable around people like them and less comfortable around those who are not. If your church is homogeneous, you might use it to better reach that group. How do you know if you should differentiate or be generic? You pray. You ask God who you are supposed to be.

Marketing in cultural groups is like aiming a fire hose at a widespread fire. If I spin around trying to hit everything, I may hit a wide swath of the flames but without sufficient force in any one area to make an impact. If I hold the hose steady in one place, I may saturate my target but totally miss many other parts of the fire. Decide to aim your focus or to broadly disperse it. Be a specialist or a generalist. Whatever you decide will determine how effective your church is at finding and touching those God called you to reach.

Do you think it is un-Christian to reach for only a certain type of person for Christ? Look at Paul; he was a self-proclaimed "apostle to the Gentiles" (Rom. 11:13). Remember that the differentiation he placed upon himself never kept him from giving freely to all people. His commitment was to "Give no offense, either to the Jews or to the Greeks or to the church of God" (1 Cor. 10:32). He simply understood his strengths of calling, reason, and relationship and used them in the way he thought best. After being all things to all people, he focused on where he felt called and where he knew ultimately he would be most effective. Paul differentiated. He focused his efforts on reaching only one lifestyle group—the Gentiles.

> After being all things to all people, he focused on where he felt called and where he knew ultimately he would be most effective. Paul differentiated.

## Moving Forward

Let's take a second to look back. What are the principles the masters of industry utilized?

Mountain Dew tapped into the principle of lingering with the masses. Doesn't that story just blow you away? They took the same approach on developing lifestyle connections as Paul did and Jesus before him—hang out with the ones you want to reach.

Nike utilized the transcending principle of inspiring others ultimately to belong. Isn't that what the Good News is all about?

It doesn't mean we promise people a rose garden. Nike promised pain, sweat, and endurance as a means to an end. What a glorious end we suggest—worth whatever we must go through to obtain this crown. Nike demonstrated effectiveness in fulfilling deeper needs by connecting with people's perceived needs.

Starbucks and a handful of great companies utilized the same principles that Solomon did. Relevant excellence in the details is powerful and the essence of creating effective atmospheres. Define your desired atmosphere. Design it. Train it. Maintain it. If you think creating an experience is not possible, think about how these companies, without spiritual help, have done it consistently over and over again. Isn't it worth the effort?

The Gap companies showed the power of differentiation they learned from years of being all things to all young people. They learned that they could be more effective as three companies than they could be as one. They learned that they could compete better in each category by focusing efforts independently on different segments of clients. In each case, they learned they could be successful being who they were. For your church, you should endeavor, through prayer, to have a true sense of calling. Who are you supposed to be? What are your strengths, your weaknesses? Who are you uniquely called and equipped to reach? Are you called to the world? To just the Gentiles? To the poor? To the rich? All of the above? Whom He calls, He equips.

How are these principles at work in your church? Write them down.

How will they be at work?

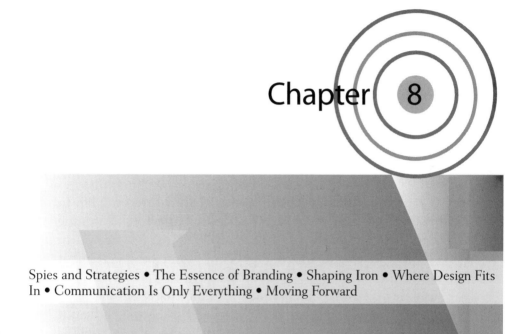

# Chapter 8

# The Branding Iron

## Spies and Strategies

Some time after I graduated from high school, a precious woman in our church came up to me and presented me with a special gift. I will never forget her or her gift. She apologized for giving me a graduation gift several months late. The reason, she said, was that she had searched to find me something perfect. She presented me with a small plaque that said, "For I know the plans I have for you, declares the LORD, plans for wholeness and not for evil, to give you a future and a hope" (Jer. 29:11 ESV).

It truly sparked something in me. I had devoted my life to Christ several years earlier and had dedicated myself at a young age to living for Him, yet I had never heard that Scripture verse. She was right. She had given me something perfect. It was worth the wait.

Initially, this verse simply meant to me that God was good and the basis of the relationship He had for me was to be out of goodness. It has many counterparts in Scripture, such as Jesus being our Good Shepherd. I began to see Him as a reliable guide—something very much needed when one is heading to college and to the "real" world. As I grew older, I also began to see Him as a planner. I ultimately saw that He wants us to plan as well. It is often through our planning that He works interactively with us. We have our part; He has His. "People make plans in their hearts, but only the LORD can make those plans come true" (Prov. 16:1 NCV).

Depend on the Lord in whatever you do. Then your plans will succeed.

Proverbs 16:3 NCV

Those who plan and work hard earn a profit. But those who act
too quickly become poor.

Proverbs 21:5 NCV

God even tells His people to plan for growth . . .

"Sing, O barren one, who did not bear;
　　break forth into singing and cry aloud,
　　you who have not been in labor!
For the children of the desolate one will be more
　　than the children of her who is married," says the LORD.
"Enlarge the place of your tent,
　　and let the curtains of your habitations be stretched out;
do not hold back; lengthen your cords
　　and strengthen your stakes.
For you will spread abroad to the right and to the left,
　　and your offspring will possess the nations
　　and will people the desolate cities."

Isaiah 54:1–3 ESV

　　With that said, this next topic is about planning and strategy.
I had the honor to visit the Democratic Republic of Congo
in West Africa in the summer of 2004. I addressed about
twenty-five hundred native pastors. I was humbled by the opportunity to speak to these men and women of God and yet I
was secretly perplexed by how I might communicate exactly
what I do. Explaining myself as a marketing executive with a
passion for churches might connect with a few, but overall,
I had a difficult time imagining that they could have enough
context to understand well enough for me to gain and hold
their attention.

　　Then it hit me. God showed me how to communicate this
unusual function of helping churches reach lives. I reminded
them of the team of spies, including Joshua and Caleb, scour-
ing over the terrain to see into Canaan; I spoke about how they

had analyzed and calculated the Canaanites, summing the data up in a report back to Moses and the Israelites. "Let us go up at once and take possession, for we are well able to overcome it" (Num. 13:30).

As I began to study this out, I saw something incredible. The very instructions that Moses gave the spies sound remarkably like what we call market research, demographics, and psychographics today. Moses told them:

> See what the land is like, and whether the people who live in it are strong or weak, whether they are few or many. How is the land in which they live, is it good or bad? And how are the cities in which they live, are they like open camps or with fortifications? How is the land, is it fat or lean? Are there trees in it or not? Make an effort then to get some of the fruit of the land.
>
> Numbers 13:18–20 NASB

Our weapons are not carnal like they were in Moses's day. But research still proves critical in knowing how to take the land for God.

I shared with them that God allows me to work with churches as a spy sent out to survey the land—to study the people they are called to reach. My job is to analyze the inhabitants and to report to the church what I see. I then have the honor to challenge them to accomplish their visions and take the land. My job is also to suggest what weapons they take into battle, to advise them that they might have to put down one type of weapon and pick up another, and that they might have to focus on areas of strength or build up areas of weakness.

Proverbs 20:18 (NCV) tells us, "Get advice if you want your plans to work. If you go to war, get the advice of others." What is a term for "advice on war"? It is strategy. Our precious Congolese brothers got my message in a way that few American ministers even do. I believe God gave many of them great strategies to expand their reach.

I know there are some that might still be having a difficult time with planning as it relates to reaching souls. If so, here's a great biblical example that proves both sides correct. There is a beautiful picture painted about church growth by Christ in John 21. You know the story, but take a second to look at it from a different perspective. The disciples are fishing their way and catching nothing: "Early the next morning Jesus stood on the shore, but the followers did not know it was Jesus. Then He said to them, 'Friends, did you catch any fish?' They answered, 'No.' He said, 'Throw your net on the right side of the boat, and you will find some.' So they did, and they caught so many fish they could not pull the net back into the boat" (John 21:4–6 NCV).

Now look a little closer than you have before. It was the disciples' plans that morning that had put them there. Some might say that this shows that growth comes at God's whim or will, and I agree it does. But think about what had brought these men into the exact position they needed to be in to simply move their nets (not their boat) to a different location. By waking up early that day and following their plans, the disciples were at the right place at the right time, just looking in the wrong direction. It is important to know that the strategic plans are there to get you in the general area; it is your obedience to God's Word that brings growth. The fish had always been there; the disciples had merely been missing them. Had they not planned and executed their plan to be in that place at that time, the miracle could not have taken place.

If your children's ministry cannot handle more children, you cannot handle more parents.

The bottom line is that strategy and planning are fundamental to church growth. If you are not prepared, you will not be able to handle the precious lives God desires you to help cultivate. He needs us to plan so we can prepare for growth, so we can be prepared not only for our actions but for people's reactions. If your children's ministry cannot handle more children, you cannot handle more parents. It is really that simple.

When we begin to look into our arsenal of marketing weaponry we can certainly see the tools we have discussed—relevance, sensitivity, and consistency—as being powerful at affecting lives. There is another weapon, that when you yield it well, will leave quite a mark. That tool is "branding," and it is a dynamic weapon used to affect perception. Wielded strategically, it is very powerful in the advancement of your church.

If you think *marketing* is a controversial word in the church world, try talking about *branding*. But the reality is, you rarely find marketing going on where branding is not also taking place. Branding stems from a school of marketing called "Integrated Marketing Communications." It is built around the aim of using all your marketing efforts to consistently communicate a strong central image and theme. If you can grasp that marketing is the management of perception, then it should be easy to understand that branding is, in simple terms, the use of defined consistency to affect perception over time.

> Branding is not just design. It is not a logo. It is not letterhead. It is the sum perception you create in the mind of those with whom you are trying to connect.

## The Essence of Branding

The origins of the concept of branding are simple. Shape a piece of iron, put it in a fire, and shove it onto the hide of your livestock. It is a by-product of sweat, fire, and pain, but it yields an indelible impression—a lasting mark that creates a sense of belonging and sets one apart.

Over time, successful branding has become a lot more complex. You cannot simply slap a logo on something and expect it to give everyone a sense of who you are. People receive such massive amounts of communication that just rubber-stamping your materials with your name is not enough to create a vivid and memorable image in their minds. Today, branding is not just design. It is not a logo. It is not letterhead. It is the sum perception you create in the mind of those with whom you are trying to connect. Design plays a part; communication plays a part; culture plays a part; and the target audience sets the plumb line.

One of our marketing giants, Nike, is known for exemplifying the essence of branding. In their heyday, back in the early nineties, they employed over 275 graphic designers on their staff—the largest in-house design department ever established. But isn't it funny, that with all those designers, you never ever saw one thing come from them that you did not suspect was from Nike before you saw the famous swoosh? Why is that? It is because Nike had such a tightly defined, well-ingrained sense of self that their designers soon learned that individual creativity was useless if it did not fit the definition of the Nike brand.

This concept has been the cornerstone of the world's greatest brands, especially over the last twenty years. You see an ad and you know whose it is before the company is mentioned—why is that? It is because they are executing their marketing strategy based on their effectively defined "self." They are differentiating themselves from others and providing an essence that draws those who favor their brand into a deeper sense of belonging.

If your church is not consistent, you run the risk of never connecting with your audience.

Think about it. When was the last time you mistook a McDonald's coffee cup for a Starbucks? You haven't. They have their own brands—their own look, their own color scheme, their own style, their own atmospheres and cultures—and they have been successful in communicating them to the public.

Corporate players as well as smart local businesses have learned that in today's media-saturated world, inconsistency does not work. Having a variety of logos, multitudes of type treatments, and general inconsistency in communication is considered schizophrenic, hokey, and unprofessional. Studies show that people are required to see a thing five to seven times before they begin to distinguish its source. Our need for repetition is a result of media overload.

If your church is not consistent, you run the risk of never connecting with your audience. Your multiple efforts might be perceived as coming from entirely different sources. Advertising agencies frequently follow up new commercials with surveys asking people what they had seen. A common trend is that a viewer can recall a specific commercial but attributes it to a different company in the same market. People generally attribute indistinguishable advertising to categorical leaders. This might mean that if the big church also sends out direct mail and yours is not distinguishingly different, you might be inadvertently advertising for them even though your church name is on it.

Why do very few churches actually embrace communications consistency, even though they see it utilized successfully by the corporate world all around them? After all, one would reason that using common imagery, design, and communication elements should save time and resources. Designers and administrative staff should be able to leverage aspects of a consistent brand identity without having to start from scratch on each project. So why don't churches do that?

Many churches simply do not see it clearly. Few churches have a strong enough sense of who they are and where they are going to make the commitment to consistency from the outset. It takes setting your sails hard. It is the commitment to make decisions with both short-term and long-term goals in mind and intact.

The essence of branding is being deliberate. The cornerstone of being deliberate is knowing who you are and where you are going. Jesus set his eyes as flint toward Jerusalem; Paul was destined and determined to go to Rome. When a church sends out an unplanned, untargeted direct mail piece, the potential for a positive response is limited to

> The essence of branding is being deliberate. The cornerstone of being deliberate is knowing who you are and where you are going.

those who are already in a "try-out" mode for a church. For anyone else, the impact is often fleeting—missing out on the opportunity to foster a clear identity and connect with recipients over time. The foundation of being deliberate is defining purpose in everything you do. Utilizing the same purpose over time creates brand.

Branding is essentially a highly concentrated use of communication. It has only one downside. To the extent a well-crafted brand can assist in growth, an un-strategic or even poorly aimed brand can keep people away and even disassociate your members.

It seems to be the default for churches to think their need in brand development is to be cutting edge. In every community that has churches vying for that position, usually only one or two ever get perceived that way and the others that try just end up looking like wannabes. Remember, the cutting edge is the first part of the knife to dull.

As a case in point, I recently had a consulting meeting with a department of one of the largest churches in the nation. They had direction. They had passion. They had a considerable budget. They had some of the greatest people in the world. They even had a defined plan of action—a cutting-edge one that was consistent with some other leading churches they were in close communication with.

As is the case in all of our meetings, we began to dissect the plan through perception management. We endeavored to understand what the church's community thought of them. We began by analyzing the deep-rooted thoughts of their community. By breaking it down, they realized that the millions they were about to spend on a specific campaign and building plan would result only in reinforcing the negative feelings that kept people out of their church. Every original instinct they had was natural. After all, it had worked for the other churches. In their case it took introspection and lingering with the masses to understand how to aim their building funds in a way that would benefit their current membership and create grounds for rebuilding ties with those in the community with whom they had become disconnected.

Developing a strong brand that truly works means taking into consideration all the things we have discussed thus far. It is not the job of a designer, a creative team, or even the communications department. It is the job of the church leadership team. Those I just mentioned are critical (if you have them) in carrying out a strategy, but determining the definition of self and setting the vision must come from the very top. If the pastor and leadership team are not championing this communication effort, do not expect it to fly. No one has a stronger sense of what Microsoft is than Bill Gates or what Apple is than Steve Jobs. The highest leader must be the crusader for the integrity of the brand. He or she must embody it and train the people to reflect it.

The essence of branding is communicating the essence of who you are in all you do.

### Shaping Iron

Following are some of the natural elements in the course of fulfilling your vision—defined as an allegory. These should also be spiritual, but I call them natural in the sense that they are not specific to the Christian cause.

- Vision: the end result, the destination port
- Mission: the purpose, why you are at sea
- Your church building: the physical boat
- Your members: its passengers
- Your leadership: its crew
- Target audience: the community or segment of the community you feel called to bring on board
- Marketing: the art of charting, tracking, and adjusting as needed to stay the course
- Brand: what others think about the ship when it passes by or when they come on board

- Branding: creating a defined sense of self in the ship's appearance and communication
- Growth: the result of casting the net from a navigated position; it is inherently both fulfillment of the vision and fuel for the accomplishment of the vision

Every organization has, in the mind of its target audience, a definition of who they are. They all have a brand. Some organizations deliberately create it and communicate it to their audience. Others miss this opportunity and therefore give outsiders the authority and responsibility to create a definition for them. For example, if your branding efforts and communication create the image that you are the "exciting new church," there is a likelihood that people, when communicating to others who you are, will use your definition. "That church over there? All I know is that it is some exciting new church. They're doing all kinds of stuff. That is what everyone is saying. I get stuff in the mail from them all the time." If your branding efforts are poor, they have no choice but to make up their own definition. "That church over there? I have no idea. One of my friends went there once and I think he kind of liked it. I think it might be decent. I'm not sure."

Which marketing message do you prefer—"An exciting new church" or "I think it might be decent"? You can either give people your definition or let them come up with it on their own.

That does not mean you can pick any definition and make it stick. If it is not congruent with who you are as a church, you are guilty of manipulation and false advertising—which will result in looking worse than if you left it up to someone else to define you. You can't just promote yourself as an exciting church. You actually have to be exciting, because if you aren't, you aren't going to fool anyone.

You can't just promote yourself as an exciting church. You actually have to be exciting, because if you aren't, you aren't going to fool anyone.

Identifying your brand and creating a branding strategy should give you the most vivid sense of where you are and where you are going that you have ever had. Difficult decisions, from promotional opportunities to carpet color, become plain, simple, and strategic. The definition of brand becomes the filter by which you, as a church, both make decisions and communicate. The litmus test becomes: is this communication or action consistent with who we have defined ourselves to be?

Branding creates a defined sense of who you are as it relates to those whom you are trying to reach. It is the definition of purpose behind things that affect human interaction. It replaces individual personal opinion with strategic intent. It predefines the desired experience, so you spend less time debating over each thing that should be done and more time focusing on moving the boat forward. It ultimately makes decisions for you.

Several years ago, I felt our firm had seen so much growth and change that it was time to recalibrate our course and reset our brand definition. Our team spent a weekend evaluating what we had learned and which direction God wanted us to go. It was a great time of congealed vision. We walked away with a strong definition of who we were. As a marketing and branding firm we felt that we were designed to be branding partners with our clients. This was compatible with most of our relationships at the time, but strategically, we decided we would no longer work on projects simply in the role of a design or technology "vendor." We were not called to just fulfill projects as much as we were called to provide solutions, being responsible to our clients for the results that were created. We determined that our relationships would be the kind that helped ministries become all they were called to be, not just what they thought they were.

Several months later, a potential client called upon us to fulfill a Web technology project. They were a significant ministry and the project could have easily earned a six-digit fee. They brought to us a list of requirements for the software and asked us to design it to their specifications. They expressly told us they did not want consulting or marketing advice (which they needed), but the project was very substantial. I sat down with Michael, our IT director, and said, "What do you think? It will take months and a heavy commitment, but look at the opportunity."

Michael looked at me and asked, "What has God called us to do? Who are we supposed to be?" This project was not consistent with our vision. We had determined who we were and had set our sails hard. To take this on, although initially lucrative, might have been devastating as it related to fulfilling our course. I knew immediately what Michael was saying. How did I even miss it? Now, we have a catchphrase in our office anytime we are tempted to become something or someone we are not called to be. "Is that our brand?" someone will ask. We gladly suggest alternatives and focus on partnering with those committed to effectual and strategic growth.

When opportunities arise or decisions come up, your team should get into a habit of returning to your brand definition. Ask yourself, "Is it consistent with who we defined ourselves to be? When we defined our brand, did we feel that we were in accord and God sealed it to be so in our hearts?" If so, the decision is made. It is the choice that best fits who you are as a church in context with those you are trying to reach.

In the next two chapters, we will discuss the tactical elements of the brand as we discuss putting the plan together. For now, it is most important to wrap our minds around the essence of brand.

Think of a prominent church in your community. Evaluate their brand. Not just their design, their brand. When you drive by, what comes to mind? Is it magnetic or repellent? Is it optimal? What do people you know say about them? Who is their target audience? What one thing could they change that would make the most difference in how they are seen? Do you know where they are headed? Are they creating interest in the community? What could they do to be a better all-around package?

How would someone on the outside answer those questions about your church?

## Where Design Fits In

Graphic design is fundamental in helping shape the brand of your church in the mind of your audience. Often, because of its use in promotional pieces, printed materials, and your website, it sets the tone for how you are perceived. It is literally the face of your church in the absence of other communication. If accurate design can resonate with your target audience, miscalculated design can alienate you from them.

So what makes good design good? For us, we measure it in effectiveness. First off, you are battling for mindshare in the recipients so you need to captivate them and draw them in. Second, it has to connect with their sense of self, need, or style. Third, it has to communicate clearly, providing more answers than raising questions.

> Effective design reels people in, conveys the essence of your brand, and provokes a predefined response

Effective design reels people in, conveys the essence of your brand, and provokes a predefined response.

People often ask me to evaluate their church's design. Without knowing the target audience, the only aspects of design I can evaluate is how professional it is, what feeling it provokes, and how clearly it communicates. But, even then, I am still partially in the dark—until I know exactly whom they are trying to reach and in what way.

A small church in the most affluent neighborhood of a large city called on us for branding and consulting services. Through our anonymous visitor review and our analysis of the church, we found the church to be about as quaint and loving as any church you could imagine. The church housed many older folks and a number of college and career age families, but no one in between. The affluent thirty- and forty-year-olds in this community went to the large, "happening" church of the same mainstream denomination just down the street.

As we honed in on the essence of who they were as a church and helped them to see whom they were most adept at winning, we began to realize that this smaller church was not going to be successful trying to outdo the Joneses. That is, they could not compete head to head with the church down the street. They had three hundred members; the other church had ten thousand members. We encouraged them to be proud of who they were. Their loving atmosphere was conducive to connecting with a growing group of young transient families that they had thought were only on the periphery of their target audience. It turns out that they *were* the target audience. The common element of this particular group was that they were young individuals and families that came from small towns and were newbies in the big city. They needed and longed for the loving "home town church in the big city feel" that this small church provided.

The consulting brought out tons of valuable information for the church, and the pastor as well as the board were elated to have their sense of self and direction clarified. Ironically, our meetings came right after the board had commissioned a new sign to be built in front of the church. The new design of the sign had been approved before our arrival—medieval lettering with a sword-cross through the word. You might ask me if I liked the sign. To give credit to its designer, it was attractive and had artistic merit. However, nothing says "we are a bunch of nice, loving, down-home folks" like having a giant sword out in front of your church.

Design, to be effective, must connect you with your audience. If you are not completely sure who you are or who your audience is, hold off on major design projects until you know. Instead of the sword, this church might have tried a cutting-edge or very hip contemporary design. In the minds of the community, this approach would have simply put them in direct competition with the church down the street. Hands down, they did not have what the bigger church had. They needed to differentiate. They needed to connect their loving church to this newbie community, not by being flashy but by being soft and real.

With that said, design has more elements than just what is professional or cutting edge. Where would a given design be rated in the scale of simple to complex? Passive to dramatic? Playful to corporate? Masculine to feminine? Traditional to contemporary? Organic to polished? I can go on and on. The important factors are the ones that affect your target audience. Do they need to see you as contemporary? How contemporary? Could you be too contemporary for a church? Where do the other churches in your community fit on this scale? Do you need to be Johnston & Murphy contemporary or Kenneth Cole contemporary? Every age group and community has its own sense of contemporary. Do you know the contemporary that your target audience embraces?

To be effective at connecting with your target audience, design needs to find its roots on the line between who you are as a church and the community you are trying to reach. Good design is not about what you and I like as church people. I dread to use the analogy of bait, but it has merit to say we have to consider first and foremost what appeals to the target audience and then design along the line of commonality that exists between them and your church. It should be about what the people you are trying to reach need to understand about you to consider you. For example, if design is based simply on the likes and dislikes of the ministry team, liturgical churches might tend to use boring graphics and highly charismatic churches might tend to put out extremely vibrant and passionate pieces. In the end, they only reinforce the stereotypes that people had in the first place. In both cases, this is hanging your personality out on your sleeve. If you reinforce the stereotypes, all you will get is people already like you. Make sure your church is

> Make sure your church is about reaching out to people with different mindsets than you—and therefore make sure your design accommodates broader tastes than your own.

about reaching out to people with different mind-sets than you—and therefore make sure your design accommodates broader tastes than your own.

Last on design, please do not simply copy other churches. You might like another church's design, but it doesn't mean it was effective for them or that it will be effective for you. Many successful churches grew in spite of their design, not necessarily because of it. To date, even the most successful churches are typically so because of synergies outside of design. You cannot even count on a flagship church to have truly strategic design. Be astute to know your target audience enough to develop your own brand to connect you with them. To be effective at design that works, consult an agency whose gifts are that very thing, or be willing to commit the time to thoroughly study layout, color theory, culture trends, design tools, professional practices, current design elements, and more for years to get your eye sharp enough. To be most effective, develop your church's brand statement before you do any design. Then stop designing based on personal preferences and let your brand drive you toward your community. After all, it should be the filter through which you communicate as well as navigate.

## Communication Is Only Everything

Welcome to the world of a million voices. So much communication is aimed at us on a daily basis that there is precious little we are able to process. Between work, family time, grocery shopping, advertising, commercials, Internet, video games, television, radio, taking the kids to soccer, and more, is it any wonder the biggest by-product of today's information overload is attention deficit disorder? Can you imagine a life where you did not need a planner to keep on track?

I am a notorious thinker. My close friends often tease me because they can sense that I am having conversations in my head. As a result, I find it uncanny how my wife is never prepared for the out-of-town trip that I swore I told her about but later realized I had only thought to tell her about. That is the difference between intention and communication. It is much like the difference between a person's heart and how they are perceived. The challenge is, until a thought is fully and clearly communicated, it really only exists in your mind. In a world where there is a battle for mindshare, the companies that have impact are the ones that communicate their message over and over again. If you missed it the first time, it will be there to be heard again.

Radio disc jockeys will tell you a similar tale about popular music. They will tell you how any hit song will begin to drive them absolutely crazy about the same time people start calling in and asking them to play it more. When a song starts to become popular, the disc jockeys are already burned out on it. They have played it over and over while listeners are hearing it for the first time.

In the church the same thing happens. Often the leadership says something once or twice and assumes it has been communicated to everyone. It is just not so. As with the radio, people tune in at different times. By the time you have said something several times some people are just hearing it for the first time. You have to repeat it incessantly if you want to make it stick. In important areas, especially when giving people the scope of the "boat" or the spiritual signposts, if you do not make an absolute routine of these essential communications at every gathering, there are people who are missing it. In today's world, you have to overcommunicate to communicate. If you are not sick and tired of saying it, it probably has not been said enough. That goes for signposts for the church at large as well as communicating brand and vision to your staff. You have to be like a broken record.

When, as a church, you create an environment where every question is answered beforehand and people need not call you to ask when, why, or how—at that point, you have successfully and thoroughly communicated. In the eyes of most people, this is overcommunication—but overcommunication is what we have to set as a standard. Doing so ascribes value to the recipients and wraps them in the warm blanket of our desire to serve them. When we communicate with a common tone, give updates, call to say hi, welcome visitors, describe signposts, avoid surprises, and explain things in advance, we create a connected partnership and a culture of trust.

> When we communicate with a common tone, give updates, call to say hi, welcome visitors, describe signposts, avoid surprises, and explain things in advance, we create a connected partnership and a culture of trust.

Explain the steps. Describe the process. Enumerate the players. Define things clearly. The absence of clarity is chaos; its presence is the foundation of community. You set the atmospherostat. You control the brand. The microphone is in your hands.

## Moving Forward

Let's take a second to look back. Planning is essential for growth. Having strategic plans will get you in the area that allows you to throw the net out for growth.

Branding is essential for knowing who you are and communicating it with integrity in every aspect of ministry. Part of knowing who you are is knowing how you come across to those you are trying to reach. Not generally, but specifically, how do you want to affect your target audience? How do you want them to see you?

Without a branding strategy, decisions fall on preference rather than on purpose. Want to have a church where decisions are never made because someone likes this color better or because church X chose that color, or because the choice of color serves the purpose and strategic intent of the church? Have a church with a defined brand. Then the color choice is based on who you are and whom you are trying to reach. Decisions become divisive where there is little vision, but they serve to unite people where there is a strong sense of church self.

Take a moment. How would you summarize your church's brand? Whom would you like to affect and how? What does it look like, feel like, taste like, and act like? Write it down.

Lastly, realize you have to overcommunicate. Define a system to overcommunicate the foundational aspects of your church every time the doors open. You will get tired of it, but people will never lack direction. Describe the flow of it in every service.

Does your church plan? Is your team united to create a defined brand experience in everything you do? Do you communicate it in everything you do? Does your staff spend a lot of time answering the same questions? Maybe you need to devote more time to providing up-front answers.

# Chapter  9

Preparing to Be Visionary • Knowing Your Destiny • Making It Plain • Moving Forward

## A Vision for the Future

As we begin to bring all of this together, remember that our entire goal has been preparing your church for growth. We haven't gotten into the specifics of promotion, such as direct mail frequency or billboard advertising. We haven't touched upon design trends and perceptual responses to color combinations. What we *have* covered is premarketing, the preparation stage you need before you begin to promote your church.

Until your church is growing steadily without external promotion (except for word of mouth), it is difficult to conclude that promotion will be beneficial for your church—it might be the opposite. Remember my claim from the beginning of the book? Most churches should not promote themselves. If your members are not actively inviting people already, there are reasons why that is happening. I would add, if the people they are inviting are not returning and staying, there are reasons for that as well. You have to learn what these reasons are. Promoting a church with these kinds of problems just asks the outside world to come in and find out for themselves why no one wants to invite people or stick around. They will leave, never to return, and will let their friends and neighbors know about their negative experience.

## Preparing to Be Visionary

Although I have included a number of biblical reflections along the way, this process is much like evaluating any secular business before promotion. New restaurants usually have a trial run for a week or so before touting their grand opening—with good reason. They need time to perfect the experience, and everyone from the chef to the wait staff to the busboys must learn how to work within the new environment. In the theater, new shows may have a number of attended dress rehearsals before the big night so they can measure the response they get from a live audience. Advertisers often spend thousands of dollars test-marketing their campaign with different groups before they run the ads. Thousands of men and women throughout the country have full-time professions in the field of "secret shopping." They are hired to shop as a typical consumer and document the good and the bad of their experiences. They also shop at their employer's competition to see the others' strengths and weaknesses—all with the intent of enhancing the experience for their clients' customers. Sounds like our principle of "sitting in their seats," doesn't it?

In the corporate world, just like the church world, there are no magical quick fixes. There are, however, principles that build upon people's willingness to invite, recommend, and attend. These principles are the same as I used in the corporate world long before I even recognized their biblical origins. Let's quickly look at business with the same eyes I have asked you to look at your church.

Take a second to think about a local store that you shopped at in the past but no longer do business with. If I were to take a poll, most of you would say one or more of the following: the staff was rude; the service was inconsistent; I was made to feel uncomfortable; they no longer offer what I need; I do not like the new manager; another newer store makes me feel more at home; or the value they offer isn't worth the drive—I can get the same thing closer to home.

Now, think about a store that you are completely loyal to—one that you are proud to be associated with and recommend to others. I would expect to hear these kinds of responses from you: people are so nice there; I always know what I am getting from them; I am made to feel so warm and welcomed; they carry just what I need; the manager greets me by name; I am proud to tell others I shop (belong) there; or I will drive across town if I have to because of how much I value what they offer.

You see? We all have the same thoughts about shopping. You don't need a doctorate to determine why some stores grow and others fail. All it takes is understanding human nature and the context between the store's characteristics and the community.

Take a second to read back over the points relating to the two stores as a parallel for churches. In the same way, there are very basic reasons why churches do or don't grow. I want you to understand these principles, because if you work with them, you will see growth.

Our goal, and my prayer, is that your churches are prepared for the growth that God desires to provide, and that is the goal you must work for. The foundation for that growth is an atmosphere that fosters it, a place where invitations flow easily and people return because of the value you add to their lives. If your church is already experiencing that growth, I am sure you have found a number of ways to "sharpen the sword." If it is not growing, ask the Lord to show you where the disconnections are.

> The foundation for that growth is an atmosphere that fosters it, a place where invitations flow easily and people return because of the value you add to their lives.

## Knowing Your Destiny

Picture your church next year, two years from now, and in five years. Close your eyes and visualize it. What do you see?

Do the other members of your leadership team see the same picture? If not, you might have a vision problem. This is not a trivial problem. This is vital. If you do not believe me, go to the Bible.

"Where there is no vision, the people are unrestrained [run wild]" (Prov. 29:18 NASB). The King James Version reads like this, "Where there is no vision, the people perish."

A vision is vital to a church. It is easy to recognize a church where there is no vision. It lacks passion and direction. Notice the Bible does not say "Where there is *not* vision," it says "Where there is *no* vision." This indicates that it is not the lack of vision (the ability to see) that is the issue, it is lack of a vision (a focus on a singular cohesive image).

So what is a vision exactly? It is a picture—a photograph—something that everyone can see. Your leadership team needs to be working toward the same picture.

Some churches, like some businesses, spend a great deal of time and effort developing what they call a "vision statement." What is a vision statement? I really have no idea. How can you write one statement that encapsulates all you see in a vision? When I look out my office window I see trees, office buildings, roads, cars, and apartment buildings. I see someone running a red light. I see six people walking on the sidewalk. I see a pharmacy and a hotel. At the hotel there are about a dozen cars in the parking lot. Of the trees I see, most are relatively robust with leaves. I see a fire hydrant. I can see a few high-rise buildings in the distance. Each one is about forty stories tall. I know there are people in them even though I can't see them. The sky is partly cloudy. The grass along the sidewalk looks to be artificially green.

I could go into the details of each of the things I see, but that would bore you. Your church does not need a vision statement. It needs a vision. Now, a mission statement or a statement of why you do things might be valuable. But a mission statement is very different. It describes purpose. You might be able to put that in a sentence. A vision that fits in a sentence does not sound very special. John had a vision in the book of Revelation. It took him about twenty-two chapters to document it.

> Your church does not need a vision statement. It needs a vision.

I challenge clients on having a vision all the time. My family, my company, and I, myself, cannot grow and flourish without one. At my business, we were recently in the middle of making a number of changes and shifting into a new direction in some areas. I knew that I had discussed these changes often with our staff and we were all excited about the new directions we were taking. As is usual with me, I had dozens of plans in my head and presumed that everyone was on the same page on everything that we were doing.

I remember one planning meeting where we were discussing what was going to happen over the next few months. My comments were based on the picture in my head that I presumed everyone could plainly see—right? Wrong. Katie, one of our department leaders, looked at me and said, "Richard, I think we all have a general idea of what you are talking about, but there are just too many details you are glossing over. We do not know enough about where we are going to get us there." She said, "What would be great is if you would tell us what it looks like so we can help you build it. Like Nehemiah, when he went late at night when no one else knew to where the walls of Jerusalem were torn down and imagined and planned the rebuilding of the city—he came back to the Israelites and demonstrated to them his vision and gave them the steps to fulfillment. It would be a great help if we knew that. Then we could make all the difference."

I sat stunned, impressed, excited, and positively challenged. How many times had I read Nehemiah in the previous few months? Katie's challenge triggered my passion. I said, "Good point! Let's pick this back up tomorrow." I went home that night and typed out the vision God had given me; I also documented the steps I saw leading up to the culmination of the vision. The next day I called my leaders to the conference room and gave them a forty-five-minute presentation on where we were going and what we needed to do to get there. My team looked at me and said, "Thank you. Now we see it with you. We can help you accomplish this."

## Making It Plain

A vision is a robust picture. You must paint it vividly for all to see. Not painting it in detail leads to as much "perishing" as not having one at all.

As we read in the Old Testament: "Then the Lord answered me and said: 'Write the vision and make it plain on tablets, that he may run who reads it. For the vision is yet for an appointed time; but at the end it will speak, and it will not lie. Though it tarries, wait for it; because it will surely come, it will not tarry'" (Hab. 2:2–3).

If you can accomplish the vision alone, there is hardly a need to write it, but if it requires the help of others, the vision must be plain so you are all running together toward the same goal.

> Not painting your vision in detail leads to as much "perishing" as not having one at all.

It is easy to diagnose a church where the vision is unclear. There is often obvious confusion, discouragement, or apathy. These are signs that the end result or even the steps to get there are unclear. When I was a volunteer youth pastor, I was asked to handle announcements from time to time by my pastor. I was glad to do it but was confused when after the first time he told me that I had not handled them correctly. I asked him to clarify, and he tried. He tried for several weeks, each time coming to me afterward to reveal hints to make the presentation better. I was frustrated and he was frustrated, and we were getting nowhere. One Sunday he decided to handle the announcements himself to give me an idea of how he wanted them done. When I saw and heard him do the announcements, I finally understood the nuances of what he was asking for and I adapted them into my routine. We went forward and all was great.

How did I finally figure out how it was supposed to be done? I saw it. That's what vision does.

With that same spirit in mind, I challenge you, as a team, to document how every connection with members and visitors should take place. Paint the picture of the perfect "greet" that a greeter could perform. Document it in story form. Do the same for nursery and children's workers. Write the visionary version of the performance of the minister, the ushers, and the music ministry. Then write what the website should do for a visitor, a member, a volunteer. Put your church's flavor into it. Make it your vision. Make it brand-conscious. Define it. Design it. Train it. Maintain it. Your volunteers and members will be happier throughout the church because they will have the understanding that they personally impact the fulfillment of the vision. They also will know they are performing their functions correctly (according to the picture of visionary execution) and can be proud of it. The leaders will be happier because the workers are stepping up to the plate to create new levels of visionary performance. There is less of a need to reprimand and counsel when the vision for what to do is crystal clear.

> Vision does not just pontificate; it defines and demonstrates.

You might think that is overkill, but I remind you of a company that breaks down the brand and visionary experience to create a picture of fulfillment for every position, function, and duty—Starbucks! Vision does not just pontificate; it defines and demonstrates. It is not about the future. It is about who and how you are determined to be today.

Another key reason to write it down is because when you find yourself in a war, the immediate needs often blind you from your greater purpose. Do you think you are impermeable to that? Think about when John the Baptist was sitting in prison.

> So John summoned two of his disciples and sent them to the Lord to ask, "Are you the one who is to come, or are we to wait

for another?" When the men had come to him, they said, "John the Baptist has sent us to you to ask, 'Are you the one who is to come, or are we to wait for another?'" Jesus had just then cured many people of diseases, plagues, and evil spirits, and had given sight to many who were blind.

Luke 7:18–21 NRSV

This is the same man who baptized Jesus. The very man who predicted and identified the Christ was now sitting in prison wondering, "Is he the one?" John's sole purpose was to proclaim the Christ. When he asked this question of Jesus, he was in effect saying, "I have lost connection with the purpose of my life."

> Jesus answered and said to [John's disciples], "Go and tell John the things you have seen and heard: that the blind see, the lame walk, the lepers are cleansed, the deaf hear, the dead are raised, the poor have the gospel preached to them."

Luke 7:22

When you really break it down, what did Jesus give as a remedy for John's failure of faith and loss of purpose? He gave him a vision. He told John's disciples *to convey a picture*! "Tell John the things you have seen." John had lost the picture he had of Jesus as Christ and Jesus knew that his faith would be restored with vision.

Vision builds faith. Vision gives purpose. Vision creates direction. Is there any wonder why "Where there is no vision, the people run wild"? In battle your staff and your church will be tempted to forget the plan God gave you—therefore you must write it down. Vision and plans are not transmitted by osmosis. They take conscious effort and attention.

*Vision and plans are not transmitted by osmosis. They take conscious effort and attention.*

## Moving Forward

As you detail your vision, you will begin to get excited with how you propose to make the ordinary things less ordinary for everyone at your church. Vision is fun! It is creative. Tracking progress, evaluating, repainting the picture, re-engineering it all—that's less fun (for most).

Here's the catch: if you are not as committed to maintain the vision as you are to cast it, your efforts will wane and your vision (and people) will get frustrated. I know this first hand. I deal with it as the chief leader of my company. It is such a challenging task that I have recruited members of my team to hold responsibility over maintaining certain aspects of the vision. I have a team member in charge of tracking our progress and one who is responsible to make sure we give frequent vision updates and provide regular vision casting to the team. Even with these in place, I still am apt to let it slip through the cracks. It is especially difficult to maintain this commitment when we go through tough times or times of transition. The vision can often get blurry, or the reality so bleak that the vision seems like a pipe dream.

As a leader, it is tempting for me to forego a scheduled update meeting if I feel like our progress is not evident; especially if this happens meeting after meeting. (I clearly admit I have done so.) The reality is that the daunting vision might be overwhelming to you, but the participants in it have only a glimpse of what you have. They need the meeting like a basketball team needs a coach and a football team needs cheerleaders. It keeps the picture of the goals before them and reminds them that God has made them up to the task by giving the vision to them.

Another challenge toward visionary progress is that as pastors and leaders, we tend to be passion-driven. The result often is that the winds blow up new ideas around the boat and stir us to pursue cause after cause—laying down one to pick up another and finding that we have lost track of the destination in light of the cause of the moment. A school, an outreach program, a building program, a new growth model we learn about, a training center, overhauling this, changing that; they are all good, but they should support the vision and fit into the vision. If they replace the vision or overall focus, the team will never know what to expect. What new wind will make us change everything we do tomorrow?

Because vision and brand go so hand in hand, it is critical to have someone dedicated to watch over and push your brand in every area of your church. After a consulting session, Jeff, a client and friend, said this about the branding strategy we were developing for his organization: "I realized that branding is not just a means to an end, it embodies every part of your ministry and becomes the fulfillment of the vision." Branding can truly do just that. If you do not track your brand consistency (the essence of self you communicate in all that you do) in your children's department, youth department, ushers, greeters, ministry, worship, website, external promotion, building logistics, and more, you cannot effectively manage the perception of who you are as a church, which is needed to accomplish your vision.

As a result, we have seen from our consulting that if a church leader (pastor, associate pastor, communications director, etc.) will pick up the torch and be the "brand champion," their odds of pulling off significant changes and growth in their brand greatly increases. Your church needs a brand champion, someone who is totally committed to the leadership, who is culturally savvy, who understands style perspective from various viewpoints throughout your target audience, and who completely understands the vision. This brand champion evaluates everything your church does against the brand. From a personality perspective, this person should not be the brand-Nazi or the brand-tyrant. This person is the

> Because vision and brand go so hand in hand, it is critical to have someone dedicated to watch over and push your brand in every area of your church.

brand cheerleader who paints the picture of brand-consistent behavior as visionary behavior to every department and who manages the external view of the church and its promotions toward the same end.

As a consultant firm, we are often called to play this role. We can perform exceptionally in this because we are not involved in the day-to-day. We can evaluate from the outside, the same way that visitors do. Yet we can, at the same time, hold the same passion and vision as the leadership team. At a larger church, you likely need an internal brand champion and an external one. You can bet that a company like Starbuck's evaluates their stores from within as well as through the eyes of third party consultants. Evaluation is simply fundamental to your commitment to create a church with a strong and attractive sense of self.

A note of advice—if you have a huge vision, you might share it just among the leadership. Telling your fourteen church members that you see a future with twenty thousand members might make them concerned for your sanity. Remember what happened to Joseph in Genesis 37? Sharing his lofty vision with his brothers got him sold into slavery. Be sensitive. Give the general membership what they can handle now and what will help them understand the needs of the near future.

> Evaluation is simply fundamental to your commitment to create a church with a strong and attractive sense of self.

When you are laying out the details of the vision, do the job completely. What will it look like for each department? What will the atmosphere be? How many visitors do you see? How will those visitors feel? How many will return? Will the sermons connect with people at every spiritual level? How do visitors feel? What will people say about your church? What will the children's departments look and feel like? How will your greeters greet? What will you be strongest at? What will differentiate you from other churches? What will your church be passionate about (meaning: what will you spend your time and energy on)? What will your church accomplish?

If you have not defined your vision, now is the time. Make sure it includes every aspect of church in which you are connecting with your congregation and with the community as a whole. Use the list we discussed in chapter 2 as a springboard.

Chapter 10

Diagnosing Your Today • Building a Bridge • Essential Action Items • Moving Forward

# Putting It All Together

We have covered quite a number of topics throughout the book: target audiences, baseball stadiums, perception management, branding, visions, demographics, and dozens more. What we have been driving toward is the understanding that marketing is a much bigger topic in the church than we have given it credit for. Marketing exists today in every church in the world, whether the churches realize it or not. In ten years from now, it will be as much of a topic as outreach is in our pursuit to win the lost. Why? Because outreach is marketing, and when we do outreach without considering core marketing principles, such as where people are in life, our shot at connecting with them is, at best, hit or miss. When we engage marketing principles to relate to people, we can reach out with a spirit of understanding that enhances our effectiveness. Simply put, the marketing conversation belongs everywhere we connect with people.

In the corporate world, everything is calculated. We know what effect a price increase has on the sale of our goods. We know our position in the market. We know how our target audiences see us. We study our product. We test market it. We navigate through it by managing perception and by branding. We know how much advertising will increase sales. We know how our clients live and think. We know what percentage of our customers purchase from us more than once—and the amount that are routine buyers. We even know what kind of people buy from our competitors.

Is knowing this information inherently bad? Is advertising because you know how many people are likely to visit and therefore come to Christ manipulative? Or rather, is there virtue in not knowing or ignoring it all? It is pretty safe to say that church leaders are less likely to understand the dynamics of what causes their churches to grow than just about any other civilized or-

> Simply put,
> the marketing conversation
> belongs everywhere
> we connect with people.

ganization. Perhaps we do not have the resources or the knowledge. Perhaps we do not want to face the reality because it can be so personal. Aren't we called to "be wise as serpents and harmless as doves" (Matt 10:16)? Aren't we challenged to "know well the condition of your flocks, pay attention to your herds" (Prov. 27:23)?

So, let's start by getting a handle on our flocks.

## Diagnosing Your Today

Just as you need to write down your vision, you need to document where you are today. The only way to build a bridge to tomorrow is to know fully where you're starting. The easy part is coming up with the quantitative data like visitor and member counts. It gets much harder when you have to analyze qualitative data, such as how you are perceived and how the ministry makes people feel. As we said earlier, people rarely are willing or able to tell you what forms their opinions. They will tell other people, but they will not likely tell you.

If you eat at a restaurant and they ask for your opinion, you might say something general, such as "it was good" or "the service was a little slow." It is far less likely you will tell them that the lighting was too bright to be romantic, yet too low for a business lunch, or that the seat you sat in had an uneven cushion, the menu did not match the décor, the salad did not seem fresh, and you had to remind the waiter a second time to bring you a refill. You will not say the red peppers in the salad dominated the flavor and gave you indigestion. You will not mention that you often avoid eating there because they have a valet out front and you feel guilty for parking yourself and bitter for feeling obligated to use the valet and spend another $5 on a tip, even though the sign says "Complimentary Valet." It doesn't feel complimentary.

Instead, you will say, "It was good." And you will probably not return.

So then, how do you get the pulse of how visitors really feel? You study them. You linger with the masses. You sit in their seats. You get perspectives from the outside. Reading books on generational trends is great, but the real issue is whether you are connecting effectively with the people you feel called to reach for Christ. The people you want to reach might not reflect the trend you read about in that book. There is no substitute for walking a mile in their shoes and seeing things through their eyes. The goal is to regain the vantage point you had before you were churched—to look with the eyes you looked with then. For some church leaders this will require taking a Sunday off and visiting your own or a neighboring church. This is probably the most difficult part of marketing, but it is perhaps the most valuable part.

A few years ago, we consulted for a church that had been, in terms of growth, stagnant for some time. New families arrived and a roughly equal number left over the last five years. In doing our consulting, when we evaluate a service, we endeavor to do so from the vantage point of the unchurched or underchurched—depending on what research we gather. At this church, we experienced a dramatically deep sermon (for the onfield "players")—a lesson that called strong believers to a level of intense responsibility and had little or no application for an unbeliever. In the course of the sermon, important topics were skimmed over under the presumption that everyone listening had the appropriate context and didn't need any further explanation. For example, we heard, "You all know what happened with Abraham's testing of obedience with Isaac," yet the description of events was never given. Vocabulary was used that only longtime believers would understand. A visiting family that sat near us left halfway through the sermon. The pastor indicated that he was not going to "water it down for anybody."

My heart sank for the people in those pews. In the meeting scheduled for the next day, it would be my responsibility as the hired gun to tell them exactly what we saw and how we felt. I take my job very seriously. My heart cried for that pastor. I desperately wanted him to fulfill the vision to which God had called him. I knew that the truth would set him free.

In the meeting the next day, I described in detail what I had seen that had created a disconnect between the message and the visitors. I explained what I had seen in the congregation's eyes and in the visitors' mannerisms throughout the service. It was a difficult but valuable reflection. The feedback I initially received was defensive, almost like, "If they don't like it, there's the door." In the back of my mind, I was thinking how well that message had come across the day before—because the visitors obviously did not like it, as they got up and left long before the altar call.

A man on the ministry team later asked the pastor to explain how he came to know Christ. The pastor got teary-eyed and said, "I was a young boy. I had always wondered about God, but it all seemed so confusing to me. I heard so many different things from so many different people. My parents did not go to church. One day, I went to a vacation Bible school with a friend at a small country church. They began to explain to me what it meant to be a Christian. In simple terms and with word pictures, I finally understood the gospel message. That was the day I gave my life to Christ." His heart began to gush with the loving touch of the Father.

Simple enough to understand. Powerful enough to change lives. That is the gospel we have the honor of declaring. When he heard his own words, the pastor finally got it. He remembered what it was like to be without Christ—to be on the outside looking in. To need to hear something that made sense more

> Simple enough to understand. Powerful enough to change lives. That is the gospel we have the honor of declaring.

than anything else in the world. He got it: in order to sit in a visitor's seat, he had to remember what life felt like without his loving heavenly Father.

Diagnosing where we're at is sensitive stuff. Handle it with tact and dignity. Be honorable. Let God work where He needs to. Be open and be supportive. Do not provide unsolicited advice. Do not step out of line. Endeavor as a team to hash this out. Bring in credible outside leaders with insight to help if needed.

Let's pull together the notes you wrote from the "Moving Forward" sections of each of the previous chapters. Summarize your church's current situation concerning each of the following . . .

- Your initial reaction to your church's current marketing status (chapter 1)
- Your initial evaluation of the various aspects of your communication (chapter 2)
- What you are showing the unchurched (chapter 3)
- How well you are connecting on all spiritual levels (chapter 4)
- The various target audiences that make up your community (chapter 4)
- How well you are connecting with your visitors and your congregation (chapter 5)
- Your atmosphere and your sense of challenge (chapter 6)
- Your calling (chapter 7)
- Your brand and your communication (chapter 8)
- Your vision-casting and your passion (chapter 9)

Look at all you wrote. Let it form a picture for you. Take the notes you have written and add to them. Let it crystallize. Create a plan from the topics above; be sure to rate your performance as well as describe it. The ratings will help you evaluate your growth. Examine and explain your church's strengths and weaknesses in each category. These are the things you need to maximize in preparing your church for greater growth.

## Building a Bridge

Now that you know where your church stands today, look at where you want to go over the next year, two years, and five years. Create visionary descriptions of your ideal church-self based on growth from your current analysis. The way to build a bridge to that future is by creating goals and tasks that carry your church toward the vision you feel God has given your team—communicating effectively along the way.

Your capacity for growth depends on the strength of the connection between who you are and who you feel called to be in your community. That potential is based on the vision your church has for the future you, but it also has to be based on the current reality. If you do not thoroughly evaluate both factors, you will find your efforts to be ineffective at best and possibly harmful at worst. Why? Because people already think of your church in a certain way—you cannot violate that, and you have to know what they think in order to change that perception. And even if they do not know you exist, you are still thought of by them as one of those churches that is not significant enough to know about, so there is still a perception that needs to be changed.

So remember, you don't get to the vision overnight. It took years to accumulate the characteristics that place your church where it is. You must utilize sensitivity and training to facilitate building the bridge to the future by using all the skills at your command.

This starts with the leadership team. Define it. Design it. Train it. Maintain it. Once the vision for where you are going is defined, your highest level of leadership needs to embrace it and embody it. Once you feel your leadership team is able to model the vision, begin to train your workers and volunteers to follow the example. Once that training gains momentum, preach from the pulpit the message of who you are and the vision of where you are going. Do not teach church marketing from the pulpit! Your congregation does not need to hear about it as much as they need to see it in action. For many of the areas of growth you envision, you might have to give your workers individualized direction like Nehemiah did to the workers on the wall.

If you need to make internal modifications to the décor or physical structure of the church, do this before you make any visible external changes. Your community has seen you in the same light for a long time. When you see progress with internal change, then take the new you public. That is when you change the name, add the slogan, repaint the outside, or release your new campaign. Do not do those things before your atmosphere and culture is set on the inside or else it will cause people to come in for a new look and see the same old thing. To be lasting and effective, change should always start on the inside and work its way outward.

## Essential Action Items

In all of my consulting I have never given the same analysis or set of action items twice. Of course, there are categorical problems and successes, trends and similarities, but no two churches are exactly alike. I do not have a template for consulting. Too many dynamics are involved for cookie-cutter answers. There are, however, levels of marketing that are necessary for churches to progress through to optimally grow. The levels are (1) connectivity, (2) branding, and (3) promotion. These levels, or stages, build on each other, and you never stop working on the first two levels, even when you are deeply involved in the third.

Let's look at level one—connectivity. Connectivity is your ability as a church to relate to, identify with, and attract the unchurched. Connection covers lifestyle issues, demographics, and psychographics. It covers where people are at spiritually and in relationship to your church. It encompasses basic human needs, as in Maslow's Need Hierarchy. It deals with the core: do we know how to become "as one to win one"? Can we make a compelling cause for Christ on the level our target audience lives? Do we do it consistently, without creating obstacles that drown out the message?

Connectivity can easily be gauged by simple statistics. How many people come as a result of invitation from a member? What percentage of your membership actively brings people? What percentage of the invited and uninvited visitors stay (move to the lower deck)? Let's take a look at an example church. For easy math, let's say it has one thousand regular attendees. Twenty-five visitors attend on a given Sunday (2.5 percent of the congregation size). Fifteen are invited (60 percent of the visitors) and ten are uninvited (40 percent). Of the twenty-five, eight return within the next month (32 percent of the visitors), and five of those eight (25 percent of the total visitors) make the church their home. What calculates here is that the upper deck is converting to lower deck at a 25 percent rate. After about a year at this rate, the church would increase by approximately 250 people. (I am doing simple math here for illustration, not amortizing it out based on growth as a percentage of incremental growth.) If we have a 10 percent attrition rate for people who move, go to another church, or otherwise stop coming, the church will be at approximately 1,150 at the end of one year. This is 15 percent net growth. Of note, if you are not converting at least 15 percent of the lower-deckers to the playing field, you will likely struggle in your inability to service your growth. All in all, in this example we're at 15 percent growth. I'll take it. I've seen and been a part of 300 percent and more, but I will take 15 percent. Below 15 percent and you are showing signs of poor connectivity. I'm actually more comfortable with 20 percent. Not until you hit 20 percent do I think we can say things are connecting smoothly. That goes for churches big and small. Just because you are big, you cannot assume you are connecting today like you were yesterday. Growth should be a healthy constant to plan for; lack of it is a significant concern.

So, what are the essentials that you must master no matter if you have 5 percent or 300 percent growth rate? How do you enhance connectivity? We've talked about them, but here they are in action item form:

- Collect and regularly analyze the data required to perform the growth example illustration above.
- Know and understand your community demographics and get updates at least annually.
- As a leadership team, commit to personal evangelism outside of the church.
- As a leadership team, commit to spending time with the unchurched; specifically those that are in your target audience.
- Watch visitors. You can read more in their expressions and reactions than they will write on visitor cards or surveys.
- Define your target audiences and know how to relate to them.
- Create a ministry pattern that speaks to those audiences and addresses the upper deck, lower deck, and playing field.
- Meet monthly (if not weekly) to discuss how you are connecting and disconnecting and how you can be connecting better on each level.
- Make inspiring others a tangible goal for every leader and volunteer.
- Bring in expert help to give you third-party perspective.

- Commit to vertical growth (winning the unchurched) over horizontal growth (Christians changing churches).
- Flush out and eliminate what disconnects people outside of the gospel in its simplicity.
- Know the kind of church you are called to be and the people you are called to reach.

This is the stage that most churches never get past. What is sad is that churches that struggle with connectivity often are searching so hard for answers to help them with growth that they look to emulate the level three promotional habits of successful churches. In doing so, they assume that the answer is promotion. It is the very opposite. It is tempting to follow the exciting creativity of the churches at level three, but until you master level one (seeing at least 20 percent growth, primarily vertical), promotion will only emphasize your inability to connect. This lesson learned is time-consuming and costly.

Another note about poor performance in this stage is that the only solution is often a culture or focus shift as a church. We have walked many a church through this. Often the biggest challenge to becoming effective is the current membership. Many of the ones who give and serve can be the greatest obstacles to change. They like the church the way it is. They like their inner circle. They like the worship the way it is. They are comfortable. God calls us to be many things, but being comfortable is not one of them. It is common that as a church commits to connectivity, a bi-level shift takes place. A segment of the congregation who values aspects of the status quo over connectivity gets stirred up and often leaves. The common denominator of this group is that they undervalue connectivity, thus they were likely never instrumental in bringing people to church in the first place. This still hurts as they represent your regulars. The social environment of the church is jeopardized. People feel like they have to choose sides. Finances struggle.

Simultaneously, the people who are sensitive to the unchurched and desire to connect friends and family to the church begin to get passionately behind the vision. Frequently the church will experience a loss in attendance and resources to emerge as a new church—no longer focused only on the playing field and the lower deck but increasingly committed to the upper-deckers and those on the outside. Since the new culture is focused on empowering the inviters and connecting with those outside the church, the long-term effect is growth.

Let's move on to the second stage—branding. Branding comes from having a cohesive sense of self as a church and effectively communicating it in all you do. Where connectivity includes knowing who you need to be to those you are called to reach, branding is, in essence, becoming that church. It covers issues like creating an atmosphere where growth occurs naturally, creating signposts for growth, and developing patterns in ministry that create challenge coupled with patience. It is about self-confidence, a strong sense of vision, and being something that inspires people to belong. It is about having a defined destination port that all can see and contribute to. It includes deliberate communication and consistent design. It is where the girlfriend principle comes into action (see chapter 6). It is where you establish a bond that is not easily broken with your membership and make them proud to serve.

As with step one, branding has some clear indicators. What percentage of your members can describe the vision of the church consistent with the leadership picture? How well do the following convey the personality of the church: logo, website, brochures, bulletin shells, direct mail pieces, signage, the building, and décor? Are communications and design decisions made on a whim or by adherence to branding guidelines? How well does your church know who it is? How the community sees it? Whom they can reach? How they can reach them? How successful are you at converting upper-deckers to lower-deckers and lower-deckers to players on the field?

So, what are the essentials that you must master to be a vision-driven, well-focused, well-branded church? We've talked about them, but here they are in action item form:

- As a leadership team, know who you are and who you are not.
- Know that your brand of church is able to resonate with one or more specific target audiences in your community—get expert third-party advice.
- Paint a complete vision—one that details all the way to the doorknobs—and appropriate it out to your staff, volunteers, members, and guests.
- Have a set of core pillars or tenants that you are committed to be passionate about as a church. These should not be generic; they should distinguish you as a church.
- Communicate and navigate by a brand definition.
- Have a vision piece (brochure) and supporting media to illustrate the vision and the brand.
- Make decisions that shape public perception with your brand as a filter.
- Have design developed to represent the brand—get expert marketing input to direct and confirm its accuracy in your context.
- Have a welcome kit that provides visitors with a sense of the size and offerings of the ship and gives them a "map" of how to get connected and grow.
- Communicate weekly from the pulpit the size (offerings) of the ship and the map of how to get connected and grow.
- Use your design style consistently. Develop guidelines for graphic use around your brand and enforce them.
- Have brand management meetings every six months, if not every quarter, to discuss how you are communicating as a church and how well your members and the community are

catching on to (1) who you are, (2) where you are going, and (3) their steps for growth with you.

- Keep statistics on volunteer rates and participation in growth classes. Track the flow and meet on it strategically every quarter (if not monthly).
- Remind people every week of the steps for spiritual growth within your church. Create a sense of continual challenge mixed with patience.
- Be consistent.

It is important in this level, as well as in stage one, that you avoid relying solely on self-evaluation. I cannot tell you how many churches will say, "We do all those things well, but aren't getting anywhere." Then, when someone on the outside steps in to evaluate, a world of disconnect becomes apparent. Expert outsider opinion is invaluable. Personally, I need it and pay for it for my company. I am too close to the action. I need someone with a different perspective. As churches, we all do. We are not islands. We are the body. It is a fallacy to assume that all the functions of the body must be performed from within your particular church. We all need each other. It brings the vision to life.

I'll take this time to mention that branding is not a consistently used term in Christian marketing. Many people (church leaders as well as designers) use the term to communicate a church's logo or its letterhead and identity package. To clarify, *brand* and *branding* are not graphic design terms. They are marketing terms. Do not let people mislead you that this topic I have covered is simply about design or that your brand is something you leave up to your designer to set. Design plays a part, but it fits into the brand, it does not drive the brand. When we work with churches to develop and implement brand strategy, the design that results has the effect of uniting the church behind the vision. It is not divisive. It does not represent a single sliver of the church's culture. It embodies the church as a whole. It resonates and inspires. It increases a sense of pride and belonging.

As you reach the point of mastery of this second level, something else interesting begins to happen. Fortunately or unfortunately, you begin to attract people from other churches. Why? Simple. Remember how I said that every true believer wants to see his or her friends and family come to Christ? What easier way than to invite them to a church that consistently demonstrates connectivity? It all the more assures that those they invite will experience a palpable, life-changing atmosphere with few roadblocks. People love to be proud of their church and share it with others. Energetic, influential people especially do. They will move to enhance their ability to connect people to Christ and stay there as long as connectivity is strong. Thus, they are not necessarily disloyal; they are just more committed to always be touching lives by plugging people into healthy Christian environments. This is not the only reason people move, but it is one more reason why the bigger church gets bigger. It all starts with connectivity and a brand to belong to.

> It all starts with connectivity and a brand to belong to.

On to stage three—promotion. This is where you take the church that is experiencing internal success and push it outward for dramatic growth. The methods of the promotion stage were not covered in this book. Why? Partly because the minority of churches are prime for it, and also because the topic is so large it deserves its own work. The one thing that I will say about it is that if you have excelled in the first two stages, you are growing already. You need to channel this momentum by promoting based on the same spirit of connectivity and brand you created internal success with. You take the same glowing church you have become and appropriate it to the community on their level—routinely, strategically, and consistent with who you are and whom God called you to reach.

## Moving Forward

How many times can your church change? Good question. Your opportunities are limited. People do not give much credibility to a church that frequently changes names, looks, slogans, and leadership. They tend to see this like a ship at sea that really has no clear destination and is constantly redirected by shifting winds. If you are going to make a change, make a commitment to make it big and make it last. If you don't, you run the risk of looking like you do not know who you are or where you are going.

Take the notes you have made throughout the book and ponder them. In each "Moving Forward" section, you should have answered the questions to detail the areas that make up your current and desired realities. Sit back and soak it all in. It may seem overwhelming, but start by painting a picture of what it would look like if you could wave a wand and make everything perfect. Start with the innermost thing—you—and make changes for the future. Make a team effort to see each element come together to form the church you were called to be. The results will be self-evident.

As you begin to manage your church's perception (market yourself), remember these critical factors:

- You can predetermine the experience a visitor should have.
- Providing consistent value produces growth.
- If your church does not minister to every level, you will not have every level. You need a steady flow of growing people at each level in order to ensure that you are ultimately equipped to service your growth.

When you first start preparing your church for greater growth, it is useful to grade each service by the standards you create in your evaluation and vision. It is important that you closely reevaluate your church on a regular basis and get opinions from outside experts. Maintain a fresh outsiders' perspective to keep you objective. Do this to ward off "like-think," a natural progression of the same people evaluating the same thing over time. As you come closer and closer to reaching your defined vision, bear in mind that you might need to set your sights higher. God will always challenge you to grow just as you will be challenging the various levels of your congregation.

If you want to see real growth in your church, you must maintain a passion to kiss the status quo good-bye. Change is a requirement of growth. No change means no growth. One of the biggest challenges I see in churches is that they commonly get stuck in the generation in which they felt the greatest spiritual impact. The same thing happens with married couples. Many couples tend to wear the same clothing style and hairstyles of the decade in which they got married, well past when the styles may be fashionable. Why? Because that is when they felt most attractive. There is a common and natural tendency to cling to an image of yourself based on a time you felt you were at your best. It happens with churches too. Some churches have music, décor, or preaching styles that are outdated, often because those in a position to decide these matters felt their deepest connections with God during those times. Let me challenge you, do not have a sense of self that clings to the past. God is doing a new thing! (Isa. 43:19). Your best times in Him are yet to come. "Sing unto him a new song!" (Ps. 33:3 KJV).

Before you start, know that you are following God's direction for your church. Document it. Set it as flint before your eyes. Set your sails hard. Stay the course. Keep your eyes on the vision. If you've lost sight of it personally or as a church, do what John

> No change means no growth. One of the biggest challenges I see in churches is that they commonly get stuck in the generation in which they felt the greatest spiritual impact.

the Baptist did and go to Jesus for renewed vision. Set it before your eyes. Run with it. If there are changes that are overdue, do them now. Your congregation will experience unprecedented growth as you prepare yourself. They will be encouraged. You will see them more excited than ever before—eager to invite friends and family and expecting a positive outcome. Do not hold back. "Hope deferred makes the heart sick" (Prov. 13:12). Do not promise change and settle for a result that is anything less than the vision.

I pray blessings and strength for you, your family, and your church. We are in this together. May God work through you to prepare your church for greater growth.

# Notes

## Chapter 6 Creating an Atmosphere That Fosters Growth

1. The Wally Interview seminar materials are copyright ROC Systems Pty Ltd. All rights reserved. Licensed for distribution through RAN ONE. Introduced in 1994 in a VHS video format, the original "Making Your Busines Really Fly" (Wally) presentation proved its extensive merits by becoming a RAN ONE institution.

## Chapter 7 Marketing Secrets of the Big Boys

1. Quoted in Nancy F. Koehn, "Howard Schultz and the Starbucks Coffee Company," *Harvard Business Review*, Nov. 28, 2001, 18.

2. Ibid., 20.

3. Ibid.

4. B. Joseph Pine II and James H. Gilmore, *The Experience Economy* (Harvard Business School Press, 1999), 1–5.

5. Ibid.

6. Ibid., 163–77.

**Richard L. Reising** is a recognized authority on church marketing and branding. He is founder and president of Artistry Marketing Concepts LLC, an organization headquartered in Dallas, Texas, that helps churches and ministries make wise use of marketing, design, and technology. He has helped thousands of ministries in the U.S. and worldwide through speaking engagements, training seminars, and consulting services.

To find out more about ChurchMarketing 101 seminars and other resources, visit www.churchmarketing101.com. For information about other marketing services, visit Reising's company site at www.artistrymarketing.com. Or, to contact Richard Reising directly, please email him at richardr@churchmarketing101.com.